SPOOKY
Southwest

SPOOKY
Southwest

*Tales of Hauntings, Strange Happenings,
and Other Local Lore*

RETOLD BY S. E. SCHLOSSER

ILLUSTRATIONS BY PAUL G. HOFFMAN

The
Globe
Pequot
Press

GUILFORD, CONNECTICUT

Text design by Lisa Reneson
Map border by Paul G. Hoffman
Map by Stefanie Ward © The Globe Pequot Press

Library of Congress Cataloging-in-Publication Data
Schlosser, S. E.
  Spooky Southwest : tales of hauntings, strange happenings, and other local lore / retold by S. E. Schlosser ; illustrated by Paul G. Hoffman. — 1st ed.
      p. cm.
  Includes bibliographical references.
  ISBN 0-7627-3425-6
  1. Tales—Southwest, New. 2. Legends—Southwest, New. 3. Supernatural. I. Title.

GR108.5.S35 2004
398.2'0979—dc22

2004054281

Manufactured in the United States of America
First Edition/First Printing

For my family: David, Dena, Tim, Arlene, Hannah, Emma, Nathan, Benjamin, Deb, Gabe, Jack, Clare, and Karen; with a special warm welcome to my new nephew Benjamin.

For my editors, Mary Norris and Mimi Egan, and for the Globe Pequot staff, with my thanks for the wonderful job they have done with the "Spooky" books.

For Paul Hoffman, with my thanks for his wonderful illustrations.

In memory of my grandparents, Loyd and Mildred Schlosser, who first took me traveling through the Southwest.

Contents

Contents

Contents

Contents

SPOOKY SITES. . .

1. Timpas, CO
2. Waco, TX
3. Fort Union National Monument, NM
4. Fairplay, CO
5. Salt Lake City, UT
6. Saguache County, CO
7. Summit County, UT
8. Crosby County, TX
9. Carson City, NV
10. Socorro County, NM
11. Castroville, TX
12. Scottsdale, AZ
13. Santa Fe, NM
14. LaPorte, TX
15. Yuma, AZ
16. Kingsville, TX
17. Bear Lake, UT
18. Smith County, TX
19. Virginia City, NV
20. Albuquerque, NM
21. Virginia City, NV
22. Sand Mountain Recreation Area, NV
23. Tyler, TX
24. Gila County, AZ
25. Santa Cruz County, AZ
26. Bernalillo County, NM
27. Austin, TX
28. Los Alamos, NM
29. Isleta, NM
30. Brazoria County, TX

AND WHERE TO FIND THEM

Introduction

When I was six years old, my grandparents took me on a driving vacation across the country from New Jersey to California. Looking back, I admire their fortitude in traveling day after day for six weeks with a very active child who was more interested in fast food and amusement parks then in the scenery. (I date my lifelong love affair with cheeseburgers to this trip, since my frantic grandmother always used cheeseburgers as a bribe to make me sit still.)

This trip was my first introduction to the American Southwest, and I still have very vivid memories of the Rocky Mountains in Colorado, the Petrified Forest in Arizona, and the Great Salt Lake in Utah. I particularly remember seeing the Miracle of the Gulls Monument in Salt Lake City and listening in wonder to the story associated with it. The Miracle of the Gulls was my first exposure to American folklore (defined in this case as the unwritten literature of a culture, since it is a true story that has long been part of the oral tradition of the Mormons). In 1848 the crops of the Mormon pioneers were threatened first by frost and then by a plague of crickets. The settlers despaired of saving their harvest, until flocks of California gulls flew in, ate the crickets, and saved the crops. It was a tale of hardship, a tale of faith, and a tale of miracles. Even as a six-year-old, it enchanted me.

Too many years have passed since that childhood vacation, but I have never lost my fascination with the Southwest. So many people from so many cultures have settled in this land. Native Americans, Spanish missionaries, Texas plantation owners and their slaves, Gulf pirates, Mormons, Forty-niners, cowboys, outlaws, soldiers, lawmen, townsfolk, ranch owners, businessmen, railroad employees, and even the writer Mark Twain have all called the Southwest home.

The Southwest is the land of the Apache and the Alamo. Argonauts with the lust for gold in their hearts tramped through this country on their way to California and braved the Sierra Nevada Mountains again a few years later when massive deposits of silver were found in the Comstock Lode. Mormon settlers came to the Southwest looking for a place to practice their beliefs in peace. Jean Lafitte, the Pirate of the Gulf, had his headquarters on Galveston Island. Cowboys shifted Texas longhorns northward on the Shawnee Trail.

The folklore that comes from the Southwest is as diverse as the cultures that inhabit it. From the mundane to the sublime, the terrifying to the hysterical, all manner of tales have been told throughout this land.

First and foremost, this is Pecos Bill country! You remember Pecos Bill, the toughest cowboy that ever lived? Pecos Bill was such a great cowboy that he could ride any living creature that ever breathed air. Once, when Bill's durned fool horse got its neck broke, he just whipped the tarnation out of a cougar, saddled it up, and tore off across the hills like forked lightening, using a rattlesnake for a whip whenever he needed to calm that cougar down. Then there's the time Bill was up Kansas way and decided to ride a tornado. Yep, he just grabbed that there tornado, pushed it to the ground, and jumped on its back. The tornado whipped and whirled and sidewinded and generally cussed its bad luck all the way down to Texas. Finally, the tornado decided it wasn't getting this cowboy off its back no-how. So it headed west to California and rained itself out.

In *Spooky Southwest*, Pecos Bill has a spooky encounter in Nevada when he visits the most haunted house in the West. Of course, Bill handles himself and the haunts in the same swash-buckling style that characterizes all his actions.

The tall tales of Pecos Bill are just one aspect of Southwestern folklore. The stories told in this region range from mystical encounters with the Blue Lady to the antics of a walking eight-foot skeleton. According to many, the Bucca still live in the silver mines, dwarfs inhabit the Superstition Mountains, and a monster sometimes threatens the locals of Bear Lake. Even the Devil has been known to visit the Southwest on more than one occasion. And for those folks searching for gold, it just so happens that I have a map I can sell you that has the *exact* location of the Lost Dutchman mine. Really.

I think what I like best about Southwestern folklore is its application to real life. I have found tales to answer the stickiest theological questions, such as "Should miners be allowed into heaven?" (The Ultimate Stakes) and "Do miracles really happen?" (Uncle Bob's Miracle). Those folks searching for true love can find answers to questions such as "What is proper post-demise dating etiquette?" (Going Courting) and "How long should I wait to marry another after my fiancé has been scalped?" (The Death Waltz). For the practical-minded, Southwestern folklore answers questions like "Which animals make the best pets?" (The Black Cats' Message) and "How dedicated should I be to my job?" (The Posthole Digger).

All in all, I continue to find myself as enchanted with the Southwest as I was the day I first heard the Miracle of the Gulls. Somehow, I think I always will be.

Sign me "G.T.T"—Gone to Texas!

—Sandy Schlosser

PART ONE
Ghost Stories

1

The Ghost on the Tracks

TIMPAS, COLORADO

The train rumbled around Jake as he adjusted the throttle. The night shift was always the toughest, in his mind. A man was not meant to be working through the night hours. It was unnatural. His wife sure didn't like it. They had argued about it just before Jake left the house to go to work. He frowned, thinking about it. He loved Miranda, but now and then she drove him crazy.

He stretched a bit and yawned, trying to stay alert. The train had driven through Timpas a few minutes ago and was on its way to Thatcher. It was not a bad stretch of track, and there was no better train in the entire Atchison, Topeka & Santa Fe Railroad. But the night run was very boring. The darkness obscured the scenery, except for a few trees and stones that appeared in the headlights.

Jake was new to this run. It was quite a popular shift with the other engineers, which surprised him. Normally, the men avoided the shifts through the dead of night, preferring daylight or early evening hours. For some reason, the Timpas run was different.

Jake was deep in thought. He was startled back to the present by a movement on the track ahead. He strained his eyes against the darkness to either side of the track. Then he gasped as the lights picked up the figure of a beautiful woman with long red-gold hair and wonderful blue eyes. She was standing near the tracks. Too near! He sounded his horn to warn her away. She would be killed! Why didn't she run?

As he reached for the brake, he realized that there was something odd about the way she appeared in the head-lights. She was wispy somehow, almost translucent. Suddenly Jake realized that the lights of the speeding train were shining right through her. His hand froze on the brake. She was a ghost!

The beautiful woman stepped into the center of the track, facing down the train. She was laughing. The train rushed right at the ghost, and Jake closed his eyes instinctively, not wanting to see the train hit her.

When Jake opened his eyes seconds later, the beautiful ghost was in the engine cab next to him. The scent of roses filled the air. He stared at the ghostly vision, bewitched by her beauty. All thought of driving the train left him. All he could think of was the gorgeous ghost. She came toward him with an enticing smile. Then she wrapped ghostly arms about his neck and kissed him. He let go of the brake and tried to wrap his arms around her, but she disappeared as soon as he moved. He looked back outside, but all was darkness save for the lights on the engine. She was gone.

Dazed and disappointed, Jake finished the run to Thatcher in a trance, almost forgetting to stop at the station.

THE GHOST ON THE TRACKS

Jake decided not to tell anyone about the ghost, fearing for his job. But he was plagued by curiosity. Finally, he confided the story to a close friend who was a fellow engineer. To his surprise, his friend had heard about the ghost before. The ghost's appearance on the train was by no means uncommon. She always appeared on that particular stretch of track after dark, beckoning to the men on the railroad crew with a bewitching smile. Sometimes, said his friend, she would come right onto the train. No one had been able to discover who the woman had been in life.

"Better not tell Miranda you've seen her," his friend advised. Jake didn't need to be told twice. Miranda was the jealous type.

Jake didn't know whether to be glad or sorry when he found out he had been permanently assigned to a different run. In the end, he decided that it was for the best. After all, sooner or later, Miranda was bound to hear about the beautiful ghost on the tracks. If he were still assigned to the run when she heard the story, she would make his life miserable.

And if Miranda ever found out that the ghost had kissed him . . . Jake shook his head. He'd be deader than a doornail. Jake knew he was lucky to be off the hook. Still, he felt rather sad. That ghost was quite a kisser!

2

The Half-Clad Ghost

WACO, TEXAS

Tess Grant stood beside the grave long after the rest of the family had gone back down the hill. Ben, her eldest son, had urged her to leave with him, but she had shaken her head.

"I need to be alone with your Paw," she told him. He nodded and left her alone.

The grave diggers were shuffling impatiently a few yards away, wanting to finish the job and get home. But Tess wasn't ready to leave. She gazed down at the flower-strewn casket in the ground, thinking about the years she had spent with her husband. Henry's eyes, she remembered, had popped right out of his head the first time he had seen her. It had taken him a few weeks to get up enough gumption to talk to her, because he thought a classy dame like her wouldn't want to associate with a dirt-poor farmer. She recollected the gentle way he had taken her hand in front of the minister and the solemnity with which he had promised to love her for the rest of his life. And she would never forget the amazed look on Henry's face the first time he had held baby Ben in his arms.

Tess chuckled suddenly, recalling the many times Henry

had dragged her away from her chores to inspect his latest invention. Henry considered himself another Ben Franklin. Unfortunately, none of his inventions ever worked. He had nearly blown them all to kingdom come more than once.

Of course, life with Henry hadn't always been a bed of roses. He had to have the last word, no matter if he were right or wrong in a matter. And he always insisted on wearing two pairs of underwear—he called them "drawers"—every day, even in the heat of summer. It made twice as much work washing up. Tess shook her head over that memory. She had fussed and fussed at Henry, to no avail. He still wore his two pairs of drawers every livelong day. At least she had gotten the last word about those blasted drawers of his. She'd had him buried in his best suit and one pair of drawers, like a normal Christian. She could take comfort from that.

Tess sighed. She missed Henry terribly and probably always would. Behind her, she could hear the grave diggers muttering restlessly. It was time to go.

"Good-bye, Henry," Tess said. "I'll be seein' you soon in Glory."

She went down the hill, and Ben helped her into the carriage and drove her home.

The house seemed empty without Henry popping in and out to get her opinion on his latest invention or to ask for her help in the barn. Of course Ben came over each morning and evening to take care of the chores, and his wife, Mamie, and the grandkids were always stopping by to see how Grandma was doing. But Tess still felt her loss keenly. Once, she took out Henry's second-best pair of drawers, laughing and crying over them as she remembered how often they had argued over his wearing two pairs every day.

That night, as Tess sat on her front porch, rocking and watching the sunset, she felt a sudden breeze chill her skin. She shivered and stood to go inside. Then she froze. Coming toward her across the front yard was a man who looked just like Henry. He had the same wide-set eyes, the same graying hair, the same way of walking. The man stopped, and Tess realized with a shudder that it *was* Henry. And she could see right through him!

Tess gave a shriek of fright. Henry blinked in surprise, then faded away. Ben came hurrying out of the barn.

"Mama, are you all right?" he called.

Tess was still shaking with fear, but she managed a smile for poor, overworked Ben.

"I just saw a huge spider," Tess lied.

Ben relaxed and chuckled. Tess's fear of spiders was legendary.

"Want me to kill it for you?" Ben asked.

"I reckon I already killed it with all my shrieking," said Tess. Ben laughed and went back to his chores.

Tess went inside and drank a cup of tea to steady her nerves. Had she really seen Henry's ghost? She decided that it had been a trick of the light.

Tess was jumpy for the rest of the night, but nothing happened. Mamie teased her a bit about the "huge spider," and her eldest grandson promised to squash it for her if the spider came back.

In the bright sunlight of the next morning, Tess soon forgot all about the ghost. But as dusk fell, the icy breeze returned,

THE HALF-CLAD GHOST

touching her skin while she washed the supper dishes. Tess turned and saw Henry standing in the doorway, looking at her. She could see the kitchen garden right through him. Tess dropped the plate she was holding. Henry frowned and disappeared. Mamie came rushing in from the parlor, where she was making up the fire.

"Mother Grant, are you all right?"

"That blasted plate just dropped right out of my hand," said Tess, reaching for the broom.

"I'll clean it up," said Mamie.

"No, child, I made the mess, and I aim to clean it up," said Tess, shooing her away. She picked up the broken shards, swept the floor carefully, and finished the dishes.

"Living with Henry was enough to drive anyone stark raving mad," Tess muttered to herself as she dried the last dish, "and now he's dead and buried and still driving me crazy! That was one of my best plates."

The next evening at dusk, Tess sat down on the porch with her knitting and waited for Henry to show up. Sure enough, she felt a cold breeze touch her skin, and a moment later Henry came walking toward her across the lawn and stopped at the foot of the steps. They stared at each other for a long moment. Then Henry frowned and disappeared.

Tess had no idea why Henry kept coming back to haunt her. If she'd gone to Glory, she sure wouldn't want to come back to earth. No sir! Tess wondered if Henry would stay put in Glory if she moved to another house.

That night, Tess told Ben she was feeling a bit lonely in the big house. Would he mind if she spent the next few nights with them, just until she got used to being alone? Ben was so happy, he gave Tess a hug. He'd wanted to invite Tess to stay with them but had been afraid she wouldn't want to leave her old home. Tess packed a bag and went home with Ben.

After supper, while Mamie was tucking the kids into bed, Tess took a stroll around the backyard with Ben. As they stood beside the swing, talking about Henry, Tess felt a familiar cold breeze touch her skin. Beside her, Ben gave a shiver and said, "It's getting chilly, Mama. We'd better go in . . . " Ben stopped, his mouth frozen open in shock. Tess knew even before she turned to look that Henry was coming across the yard toward them.

"Paw," gasped Ben.

Tess shook her head as Henry's ghost stopped in front of the swing. He stared at Tess, and she stared right back at him. Ben looked back and forth between both his parents, one dead and one alive. Tess could tell Ben wanted to speak but didn't know what to say.

Tess was beginning to find the situation annoying. If Henry was going to haunt her, at least he could tell her what he wanted. Tess put her hands on her hips and said, "What in the name of the good Lord do you want, Henry?"

Henry cocked his head, considering her question just as he had often done in life. Tess began to tap her toe, a sure sign that she was getting ready to box Henry's ears if he didn't speak up. Henry flinched a bit and said, "Honey, gimme another pair of drawers, please. I feel naked up here in heaven, wearing only one pair."

"For mercy's sake!" gasped Tess. "You came all the way back from heaven for another pair of drawers?"

Henry grinned sheepishly and nodded.

"Well, all right. Ben will put another pair on you tomorrow morning. Won't you, Ben?" Tess turned to glare at her eldest son.

Ben swallowed hard. He didn't want to dig up his father's grave, but he knew better than to argue with his mother when she spoke in that tone of voice.

"Yes, Mama," he said.

"There! Does that suit you, Henry Grant?"

"Thanks, honey," Henry said, starting to fade away.

"Henry Grant, you come back here this instant," said Tess. Henry's ghost solidified immediately. He too knew not to mess with Tess when she spoke in that tone of voice.

"What you want, honey lamb?" Henry asked soothingly.

"Are you done hauntin' me?" Tess demanded.

"Yes, ma'am. Now that I got me my second pair of drawers, I'll be fit for company up in Glory. I'll be waiting for you there," said Henry.

"Good. I'll meet you there by and by," said Tess.

"You'll like it there, Tess my girl!" Henry cried enthusiastically, becoming almost solid in his excitement. "I've got a great big laboratory and all kinds of chemicals and tubes and wire and things. I'll be the greatest inventor in heaven, wait and see."

"Lord have mercy," said Tess. "You'd best be getting started then."

"Yes, indeed!" Henry said. "See you later, honey lamb!"

Henry disappeared, and Tess sat down on the swing.

"Mama!" gasped Ben. "Was that really Paw?"

"It was your father, all right," said Tess grimly. "No one else would come all the way back from heaven for a second pair of drawers!"

Ben helped Tess off the swing, and they walked back to the house.

"Now, don't you forget to put that second pair of drawers on your father tomorrow," Tess said to Ben as they entered the house. "Or he'll be a-hauntin' us 'til kingdom come."

"I will, Mama," said Ben.

Tess shook her head in disbelief. "I don't know *what* the good Lord was thinking when he gave Henry that laboratory. Ben, my boy, I just hope the good Lord put Henry in the farthest corner of heaven, or there won't be any pearly gates left by the time we get there!"

3

The Death Waltz

Johnny and me (my name is Jacob) grew up together on a ranch owned by his daddy. My pa was a cowboy turned ranch manager who handled the everyday duties of the ranch. Me and Johnny used to run wild when we were little. We loved to pretend that we were soldiers, and we always said we would join up as soon as we were old enough.

Johnny's daddy wasn't too happy when his only child joined the military. My pa didn't care what I did, as long as I was a credit to the family. My mam was so proud, she cried when she saw me in my uniform.

Johnny's money paved the way for him, and he soon achieved the rank of lieutenant. I didn't advance as high as Johnny, since I had to work my way up through the ranks. But Pa always said I had a good head on my shoulders and I was a survivor. I saw quite a bit of action in the wastelands beyond Missouri, and I did my duty to the best of my abilities. It was a pretty rough life. You never knew which of your friends might be shot or when an Apache war party might surround you and you'd have to fight for your life.

Then one day my captain promoted me to sergeant, and the next thing I knew I was stationed at Fort Union. Fort Union was a mighty fine place to be. It was the only place for miles around where there was any kind of social life. I saw some very pretty women the first day I arrived.

It didn't take me long to discover that Johnny was also stationed at Fort Union. Johnny came to the barracks as soon as he heard I had arrived, and we talked 'til sunset and beyond. Johnny was still the same eager boy he had been when he joined the military. My mam had worried that having too much money might make the military too easy for Johnny. She always said he would have a hard time growing up. I'd laughed over her words at the time, but I could see she was right. I felt a hundred years old next to Johnny, who'd not seen any heavy action. Johnny laughed at me and called me a grizzled old soldier. I laughed back and called him "sir."

As soon as Johnny mentioned Celia's name, I knew he had it bad for her. To hear him talk, Celia was the most amazing woman who had ever walked God's green earth. She was the sister-in-law of the captain, and all the young men on the base were infatuated with her. Celia was the prettiest of the eligible ladies that graced Fort Union society, and she was filled with a spirit of adventure.

Johnny alternated between elation when Celia talked with him and despair when she flirted with another man. I watched their courtship from afar, finding it difficult to spend time with Johnny since he outranked me. The other men would think I was courting favor with the high-ranking officers if Johnny and I were too friendly. I don't think

Johnny really noticed the distance between us. He was too taken up with Celia.

There was something about Celia that I didn't like. I never mentioned it to Johnny, but I thought she was too much of a flirt. I wished Johnny had fallen for a nicer woman. I confided my thoughts to Marge, one of the other girls who attended the socials at Fort Union. Marge was rather plain and didn't sparkle at the dances like Celia did. But she was real smart, and her eyes were beautiful when she smiled. Marge agreed with my assessment of Celia, but she didn't reckon there was much we could do for Johnny. She thought that Celia might marry Johnny, since he was rich.

One night at a dance, I asked Marge to marry me. She blushed as red as a rose and said yes. Well, sir, our engagement became the talk of the party. Celia didn't like it one bit. She'd always supposed that she would be the first of her set to marry.

Then the dance was interrupted by a messenger reporting an Apache raid, and Celia clung shamelessly to Johnny. She begged him not to go, even though he was the lieutenant put in charge of the mission. Well, sir, Johnny proposed to her right then and there, and Celia accepted, going as far as promising that she would wait for him, and that if he didn't come back, she would never marry. It was a touching scene, and it completely eclipsed Marge's and my engagement, not that we cared. I doubted Celia's sincerity, but Johnny just ate it up.

I was assigned to Johnny's troop, so I had to leave too. Marge and I had a private good-bye. I told her real firm that if I didn't come back, she was to marry a good man and be happy. Marge laughed rather tearfully and told me I'd just better come back.

We started out the next morning and had a rough week tracking down and fighting the Apaches. Johnny split up the troop and gave me command of the second group. My group reached the rendezvous point with no casualties, but only half of the other group arrived, and Johnny was not among them. They'd been ambushed by the Apaches. I had to take command of the troop. We searched for survivors but never found Johnny's body. As soon as I could, I ordered the men to turn for home.

Celia made a terrible, heart-rending scene when she found out Johnny was missing. It turned my stomach. Marge made no scene when I came to her door, she just held me close for a long time. We were married a week later, in a small wedding at the minister's house. I moved into married quarters and was as happy as I'd ever been, except when I thought of Johnny.

The captain promoted me to lieutenant and said he was proud of the way I'd handled the troops. He let me take some leave to report Johnny's death to his family in person. I took Marge with me and introduced her to Pa and Mam. They loved her right off, and so did Johnny's folks. We told them Johnny had been engaged to a woman named Celia but didn't tell them what she was like. Johnny's mama cried and said she was glad he'd found someone to love him.

About a month later, a rich, handsome lieutenant from the East arrived at Fort Union. Celia took a real shine to him. Johnny was apparently forgotten, along with her promise to him. It wasn't long before Celia and the lieutenant were engaged and started planning a big wedding. Nothing but the very best would suit Celia, and her bridegroom had the money to indulge her. Everyone in Fort Union was invited to the wedding. I didn't want to attend, but Marge said it would look strange if I didn't.

The weather was perfect on their wedding day. Everyone turned out in their best clothes for the ceremony and celebratory ball. Marge was looking downright beautiful in a blue dress that matched her eyes. We danced every dance. Marge insisted on it, saying that soon she would be too big to dance—she'd told me just that morning that I was going to be a father, and I was walking on air.

We were waltzing around the ballroom when the door flew open with a loud bang. A gust of cold air blew in, dimming the candles, as a heart-wrenching wail echoed through the room. The music stopped abruptly, and everyone turned to look at the door. Standing there was the swollen, dead body of a soldier dressed in an officer's uniform. The eyes were burning with a terrible fire. The temple had a huge gash from a hatchet blow. There was no scalp. It was Johnny.

The whole crowd stood silent, as if in a trance. No one moved, no one murmured. I wanted to cry out when I recognized Johnny, but I was struck dumb like the rest of the wedding guests.

Johnny walked across the room to where Celia stood, frozen in horror. He took Celia out of her bridegroom's arms and looked at the musicians. As if in a trance, they began to play a horrible, demonic-sounding waltz, and Johnny and

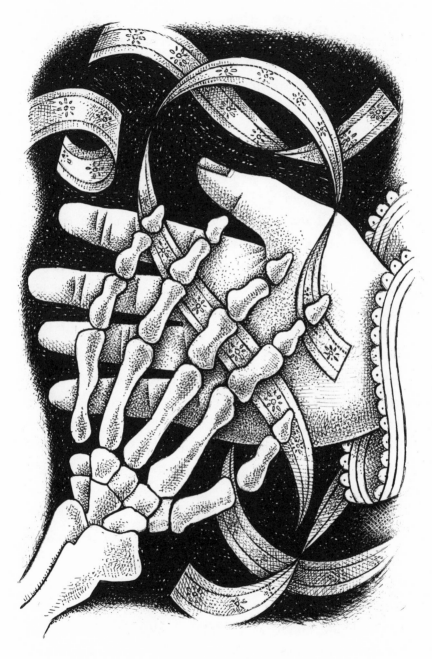

THE DEATH WALTZ

Celia began to dance. They swept around and around the room, doing an intricate waltz. As Johnny held Celia tight against his chest, a deathly pallor crept over her face, and her steps slowed. But still Johnny held her tight as he waltzed. Soon Celia's eyes bulged. She turned as white as her gown, and her mouth sagged open. With one small gasp, she died in Johnny's arms.

Johnny immediately dropped Celia's body on the floor and stood over her, wringing his blood-stained hands. He threw back his head and gave another unearthly wail that echoed around the room. Then he vanished through the door.

We all found our voices and gasped and exclaimed as the bridegroom ran to Celia and knelt beside her, wringing his hands in the same manner as Johnny. But his cries were all too human.

I took Marge home right away, afraid of what the terrible scene might do to her and our baby. Then I went to the captain and asked permission to take a small detail back to the place where our troop had been attacked by the Apaches. He sent a dozen men with me. We combed the area and finally found Johnny's body. It looked exactly the same as it had appeared the night of the wedding. We brought Johnny back with us and buried him beside Celia.

Celia's bridegroom went back east and never returned. I resigned my commission and took Marge back to the ranch. Pa started training me to take over his job as ranch manager, and Johnny's folks welcomed me and Marge into their home and hearts. Eight months later, Marge and me had a bouncing baby boy. We named him Andrew after Johnny's daddy, and we asked Johnny's folks to be his godparents. They doted on little Andrew as if he were truly their own grandson.

Johnny's parents still keep his portrait on the wall, and when they speak of him, they talk about his antics as a child and his heroics as a young man. No one ever mentions Fort Union, Celia, or Johnny's death.

4

Going Courting

Being the only sheriff in a rough-and-tumble mining town like Fairplay keeps me on my toes, but every once in a while I need a break, just like any other man. In the last month I'd captured and hung a couple of low-down horse thieves, straightened out the town drunk, and even found a lost little girl who wandered away from her home. So I figured I deserved some time to myself. I was going courting, and the object of my affections was Sylvie, a lovely young girl living over in Leadville. She was the minister's sister, and I was aiming to make her the sheriff's wife just as soon as I passed muster with her brother, the preacher.

I'd settled in Fairplay because I liked the name so much. As sheriff, it was my job to see that everyone got their fair play, so to speak. The town of Fairplay is located in the center of Colorado, at an elevation of 8,500 feet. It lies in a valley, surrounded on all sides by mountain ranges and supplied by water from the north, middle, and south forks of the South Platte River. About the time the first gold was discovered in Taryall Creek in 1859, you could still find huge herds of game and colonies of beaver, muskrat, otter, and bobcat right here in the valley. The town of Fairplay grew out of a small mining camp at the junction of Beaver Creek and the South Platte. The original inhabitants named the camp "Fair Play" because they aimed to offer the same in good measure to all comers. They were mighty angry at being locked out of the diggings in "Grab-all," which was their name for Taryall and the other mining towns.

I'm a lawman, not a miner, but I staked a claim in a lonesome gulch and did some panning on my days off. I even found myself some silver that I put away for a rainy day. I never mentioned my find to anyone. I don't need much in the way of worldly goods, though when I marry Sylvie, that money will come in handy.

A hearty greeting from my good friend Nathan broke into my thoughts. I stopped to answer him, and we chatted for a few moments before Nathan mounted his horse and rode away.

Time was getting on. If I did not hurry, I would not have time to see Sylvie that evening. I rushed homeward through the bustling street, dodging a miner's cart, waving to the fellows shopping at the mercantile, and tipping my hat to Mrs. Johnson as I hurried along. Just then, someone bumped square into me. It was J. Dawson Hidgepath, one of the new miners in town. We teetered back and forth a bit and I steadied the tiny, round chap before he fell over completely. J. Dawson bobbed up and down on his toes and took off his hat.

"My apologies, sheriff. This unfortunate accident was entirely my fault. I fear I was woolgathering and did not see you walking thither." J. Dawson spoke with a hint of a Boston accent. His words were pompous but delivered with such an anxious smile that I forgave him. J. Dawson couldn't help the way he talked. He'd been born into some la-dee-dah rich family back East and had been a less-than-successful banker before traveling to the western territories to make his fortune. I surveyed him. He was gussied up and clutching a rather battered bouquet of flowers. Apparently, I was not the only one going courting this evening.

J. Dawson had two goals in life: to find a rich vein of gold he could stake out for himself and to find a bride. It seemed he hadn't been too popular with the eastern ladies, and I could hardly blame them. J. Dawson was short, round, bald, and resembled a billiard ball when he slicked back the few remaining hairs on his head. So far, he hadn't had any luck either with the gold or the western ladies. His smooth, eastern manners seemed rather sissy and irritating among the rough miners and rowdy residents of this wild western town. He'd courted the schoolteacher, the local farmers' daughters, and even took to visiting Lou and a few of the other entertainers at the saloon in Alma. To no avail.

J. Dawson looked ruefully at his handful of squashed flowers as he apologized to me. I grinned and said: "Who are you courting today, J. D.?"

J. Dawson's lips pursed in annoyance at my casual nickname. He hated to be called anything but J. Dawson. But I was one of the few citizens of Fairplay whom he liked, so he put up with my jokes.

"I am paying a visit to Beth Ann Sawyer," J. Dawson said, flushing a little. "She wanted to hear about the latest styles in Boston."

Beth Ann had come west with her father and kept house for him before becoming a schoolteacher in the next town. She was a pretty, flirtatious thing who showed no particular favor to any of her many beaus.

"Have a good time," I said, patting him on the shoulder before hurrying home to get slicked up for Sylvie.

The minister was home that evening and was kind enough to stable my horse for me so I could spend a few moments alone with Sylvie before he joined us in the parlor. The talk became general, and I mentioned J. Dawson's newest conquest. I'm afraid we laughed a little over his persistent courting of the local ladies.

I was sorry later about that laughter, as harmless as it was. The next day, one of the miners came running into the jailhouse to tell me that they had found J. Dawson's lifeless body at the bottom of a cliff. He had fallen several hundred feet off the mountain, where he was prospecting for gold. We buried him in Buckskin cemetery, and the minister said a nice service over his remains.

I'm afraid that was the last I thought of J. Dawson Hidgepath, until two days later, when the sheriff in Alma called me out to their local saloon to view the remains of the same J. Dawson Hidgepath. J. Dawson's body was lying in the bed of one Lou, a lady of the evening that he had courted a few months back. Lou was busy calming her hysterics down in the bar with whiskey, a process that seemed to have been taking place for over an hour. Although Lou was fairly well plastered when I interviewed her, her story was simple: She had been sleeping it off after a busy night among the miners when she awoke to find J. Dawson lying beside her, dead. Naturally, this had upset the girl a great deal. I thought it was a dirty trick played on Lou by one of her ex-suitors, and I asked Lou if any of her callers held a grudge against her. But she swore on a stack of Bibles that none of her gentlemen would do such a thing. I didn't believe her at the time, but there wasn't any way I could prove she was lying. I took J. Dawson back to Fairplay with me and buried him again.

A week later, Beth Ann's father came storming into the jailhouse and dropped the corpse of J. Dawson at my feet. Mike Sawyer wanted to kill someone, but since the offender was already dead, he contented himself with yelling bloody murder at me, as the upholder of the law. It seemed Beth Ann, too, had awakened to find J. Dawson next to her in bed, and the poor girl had screamed herself hoarse and then fainted dead away. I promised her father I would find the culprit and have him horsewhipped. Sawyer went away, still in a rage, and I grimly set myself out to locate this trickster who was torturing J. Dawson's lady friends.

Naturally, no one knew anything. The miners, to a man, avowed their innocence, and the shopkeepers and businessmen who made their fortune off the miners claimed ignorance of the whole matter. They treated the matter as a joke, speculating privately on who was digging up poor old J. Dawson.

Three days later, I was awakened by someone banging on my door. I drew on some pants and ran to open it. The local school-teacher was standing on the doorstep, wringing her hands.

"J. Dawson," she gasped. "He . . . he . . . " She pointed toward the schoolhouse.

I rushed down the road and stopped a few feet from the schoolhouse door. J. Dawson was propped against the doorpost, a piece of paper held in his hand. After being dead two weeks, he was not a pretty sight. I took the paper out of his hand and read it quickly. It was a love letter. Behind me, the schoolteacher stood looking at the ugly sight. I showed her the letter, and she readily told me that J. Dawson had courted her almost a year back.

"I am afraid we didn't suit," she said primly. Looking at her, as pretty as a picture and as tough as nails underneath, I quite agreed. J. Dawson had never been enough of a man for her. I removed the corpse, had the body buried as deeply as possible, and piled heavy stones atop the grave. I renewed my efforts to find the culprit and kept watch over the graveyard a few nights, hoping to catch the prankster in the act. I guess I scared the man off, because things settled down, and J. Dawson remained in his grave for several weeks.

Then came a spate of activity. J. Dawson was found sitting on the porch of the local advocate's house, clutching flowers with a note addressed to the eldest daughter. Next, he was found sitting on his favorite barstool, with a box of sweets addressed to one of the pretty lady entertainers. He visited several prosperous businessmen's daughters with love letters and bouquets of wildflowers. After spending nearly every night at the graveyard, I had to hire a couple of local boys to watch for me, since I was getting too tired to carry out my regular duties.

One night I was roused from my bed by Jed, who had been on watch. The boy was babbling. "He came up out of the grave! I swear, sir! It was J. Dawson. He came out of the grave and started picking wildflowers. I ran right over."

"Don't talk nonsense," I said sharply, assuming the boy had fallen asleep and dreamed the whole thing. I grabbed his arm and marched him to the graveyard. The earth of J. Dawson's grave was disturbed. I swore sharply. Jed and I started searching through the town, looking for J. Dawson and the man who had unearthed him again. He had visited just about every single woman in Fairplay. Where would he go next?

Then I thought about Sylvie. J. Dawson had tried to court her shortly after he arrived in Fairplay. I had run him off, and he had apologized profusely, but everyone knew he had tried to court the sheriff's girl.

I saddled my horse and rode quickly toward Leadville. It was dawn by the time I neared the minister's house. As I rode up to the low picket fence, I saw a figure trudging up the path toward the front porch. My horse reared slightly, frightened. I reined him in and sat staring in horror at the upright figure of J. Dawson Hidgepath as it climbed the porch steps, unaided by any human. My flesh crawled and my stomach heaved. J. Dawson held a posy of wildflowers in his decaying hand.

Just then, Sylvie came out of the chicken coop with a basket full of eggs over her arm. She saw me by the gate and gave me a surprised wave. Then she registered the terror on my face and turned to look at the house. She saw J. Dawson raising his rotting hand to knock on the door. She gasped, dropped the basket of eggs, and swayed.

I don't remember jumping off my horse, but I must have, because I reached Sylvie in time to keep her from crashing to

GOING COURTING

the ground. I shouted for help, and the minister came bolting out the front door and fell over J. Dawson. He gave a terrified yelp, swore—something I never heard him do before or since—and came running down to join me. Together, we carried Sylvie into the house through a side door.

She awoke almost instantly, and we told the minister what we had seen. To his credit, he believed us immediately.

"I have had enough of his shenanigans," the minister said. "If he is going to behave like he belongs in a cesspool, than that is where he belongs!"

He marched out the front door. Sylvie and I followed to see what he would do. The minister grabbed the moldering body of J. Dawson Hidgepath and dragged it down the road to an old outhouse that stood near an abandoned miner's shanty just outside town. He ripped off the wooden seat and threw J. Dawson down into the muck inside.

Together, we tore down the outhouse and buried the cesspool with J. Dawson inside. Sylvie insisted we erect a rough wooden cross over the grave. Then we went back to the house, and all three of us had a stiff drink. I am not sure if it was the drink or the act of burying the troublesome corpse of J. Dawson Hidgepath that broke down the barriers between us, but the minister was very friendly to me over breakfast. He was so friendly that I took my courage in hand and asked him right then and there if I could marry Sylvie. He said yes.

After the minister's cesspool treatment, the corpse of J. Dawson Hidgepath didn't dare show its moldering face again. Sylvie and I were married by her brother in the church in Leadville and have lived very happily in Fairplay ever since.

5

The Ghost of Jean Baptiste

SALT LAKE CITY, UTAH

It was early spring, and my husband, Tom, and I were visiting friends in Salt Lake City. We had retired a year ago and had been traveling ever since, doing all the things we had said we wanted to do. Karl and Inga were living in a tiny apartment in the city and had no room for guests, so Tom and I were staying at a hotel near the lake.

One evening, Tom and I slipped away to have some time alone together. We drove to the lake and walked hand in hand along the southern shore, sweethearting like a pair of teenagers, though our youngest child was out of college.

As we walked, the air seemed to grow colder. I shivered a little, and Tom put his arm around me.

"It's getting pretty chilly," he said. "Do you want to go back to the hotel, Sally? We're supposed to meet Karl and Inga for dinner at eight."

I nodded. We had been so absorbed in one another that I had not realized how dark it had grown, nor how far we had walked. We had just turned to go back when I was struck by a wave of coldness that made me stop with a gasp. Tom and I exchanged frightened glances as the gentle evening breeze rose, moaning around us in the growing twilight. I was filled with a terrible sense of dread.

The wind died abruptly, as if switched off, and all the sounds around us—the swish of the wind through the grass, the lapping of the lake, the chirruping of the birds—became muted, as if heard through glass. As we stood facing the lake, we both saw a man materialize seemingly out of nowhere. He gazed at us for a moment, with a look of loathing that made my skin crawl, then he turned and began walking slowly along the lakeshore. I noticed he had an old-fashioned woman's dress and a pair of men's trousers clutched in his hands. The clothes were soaking wet and appeared rotted, as if he had plucked them out of a garbage heap. My heart was beating so fast I thought it would pop right out of my chest, and I clung tightly to Tom. Neither of us moved. We watched the man walking along the shore. Then before our eyes, he vanished into thin air.

The breeze picked up, and the soft sounds of nature returned as soon as the man disappeared. I gave a small cry of terror, and Tom hugged me close. I could feel him shaking.

"Let's get out of here," Tom said hoarsely, and pulled me away. We almost ran to our car, eager to be far from that haunted shore. Neither of us spoke until we were safely back in our hotel room.

"Who or what was that?" Tom asked me as we dressed for dinner.

"I think it was a ghost," I said.

Tom shook his head in wonder. "I don't believe in ghosts,"

he said. "But after seeing that man appear out of nowhere and then vanish . . . "

He went into the bathroom.

"What else could it have been?" I called after him.

"I don't know," Tom said, and began brushing his teeth.

We met Karl and Inga at the hotel restaurant and told them the story over dinner. Karl and Inga exchanged glances when I described the ghost.

"I think you saw the ghost of Jean Baptiste," said Karl.

"Who is Jean Baptiste?" I asked.

"I have heard that Jean Baptiste was the grandson of Sacagawea," Karl explained, "the woman who guided Lewis and Clark on their expedition. He was mistreated, so the story goes, because he was a half-breed, and had come to Salt Lake City seeking anonymity. He lived in a small house with his wife and worked for five years as a grave digger."

The story, according to Karl, went like this: In 1862, a man named Moroni Clawson, who was a prisoner in Salt Lake City, made a jail break and was shot by the police. Clawson was buried in the local cemetery at the expense of the county, and one of the policemen purchased decent burial clothes for him. A few days later, Clawson's brother came to take his brother's body back to the family's hometown. When they exhumed the body, it was found dumped face down in the casket, naked. The family was outraged, and the police began investigating the matter.

Attention soon focused on Jean Baptiste, the grave digger. The police visited his home. While interviewing Jean Baptiste's wife, they discovered boxes full of burial clothes and shoes. Jean

THE GHOST OF JEAN BAPTISTE

Baptiste had robbed over three hundred graves during his career, not only taking the clothing but selling stolen jewelry to the local secondhand stores. At the time of his arrest, Baptiste was wearing the suit in which a local saloon keeper had been buried.

Outraged citizens came to the city hall to identify the clothing found in Baptiste's house. He had robbed the dead of all ages, from children to grandparents. Angry mobs stood outside the jailhouse, threatening to lynch him. Baptiste was even shunned by the other inmates. After he was convicted of grave robbery, the authorities had Baptiste secretly exiled to Antelope Island because they could not guarantee his safety in prison. He was later moved to Fremont Island, to prevent him from wading ashore.

"Brigham Young, the former territorial governor and head of the Mormon Church, finally preached a sermon to the worried people of the city, assuring them that their loved ones would appear at the resurrection wearing the clothes in which they had been buried. This helped allay many fears. The police had the clothing buried in a single grave in the cemetery.

"Three weeks after he was taken to Fremont Island, Jean Baptiste disappeared and was never seen again," Karl said. "Some people believe he built a raft and escaped the island. Others say he committed suicide. It remains a mystery to this day. I've heard rumors that his spirit haunts the south shore of the Great Salt Lake, but you're the first people I know who have actually seen him."

"It's not an experience I want to repeat," I said grimly.

"Nor I," Tom agreed.

We never went walking along the Great Salt Lake again.

6

The Phantom Train

SAGUACHE COUNTY, COLORADO

A couple of months ago, I was assigned to the Green River run, the route over Marshall Pass. It is quite a track, switch-backing over the pass, with a drop of 12,000 feet down to the sea. I was pulling a passenger car behind me and, thank the good Lord, had not had any troubles during the first few months of the new run.

But there came one night in early winter when I boarded the train with trepidation. There was something about this chilly evening that had me spooked. I had been engineering on trains since I was a young fellow, and I had never had a feeling like this before. The night was very still. The voices of the pas-sengers seemed muffled in the frosty air. The track had never seemed quite so dark before, and there were reports of a defective rail a little way up the track, followed by an unsafe bridge. It was not a good night to be making the run to Green River. A light snow began falling as we pulled out of the depot, and it got heavier the higher we climbed.

We had just left the first line of snowdrifts behind when I heard a sharp whistle echoing outside among the rocks and the icy snow. At the same moment, the gong sounded in my cab. I instantly applied the brakes, wondering what was wrong.

The conductor came running into the cab, shouting, "Nelson, what did you stop for?"

"You signaled me to stop," I shouted back, annoyed.

The conductor shook his head frantically. "I gave no signal! We need to get moving. Number 19 will be at the switches before us if we don't hurry, and there's a wild train coming up fast behind us!"

In railroad parlance, a "wild train" was one that was running without any schedule or time card. Wild trains caused accidents and often death. Just what I needed on an already difficult run.

I drew the lever at once, sanded the track, and started the heavy train back up the mountain. Behind me, I could hear the whistling of the wild train coming closer and closer. The whistle was sounding danger signals, and I leaned out the window as we turned a curve, trying to get a look at the wild train through the falling snow. It was traveling much faster than we were, and I broke into a cold sweat as I realized that if I didn't speed up, it would crash right into us.

I pulled the throttle wide open, and the train lunged through a large bank of snow that had drifted over the track. Snow sprayed every which way, and the cars lurched, but we made it through. The falling snow made the visibility poor, and I could barely make out a second deep drift ahead. This was where the defective rail had been reported. I had been planning on moving slowly and cautiously over the spot, not wishing to cause an accident. But the threat from behind us was greater than any defective rail.

I shouted to the fireman to keep pumping more coal on the fire. The poor man was drenched with sweat, but he put on a bit more speed, and soon fire was belching from the smokestack. The conductor came running in, wringing his hands.

"They are gaining on us, Nelson," he panted. "The passengers are glued to the windows. They think the engineer behind us is mad, and I agree with them!"

"Try to keep everyone calm," I said firmly, and sent him back to the passenger cars.

As we crossed the summit, I shut down the steam and let gravity pull us downward. I looked back as best I could, trying to gauge where the wild train was. I saw it immediately through the wind-whipped snow, rapidly closing the gap between us. It had much larger driving wheels on the rear engine. I could also make out a dim figure on top of the cars.

"Pull back," I shouted, waving frantically at the figure.

As we rounded a sharp turn in the tracks, I got my first clear look at the wild train. It was barely two hundred yards behind us now, and the engineer leaned out of the window. I could hear him laughing madly. His face was whiter than the falling snow, and his eyes blazed at me.

We were roaring down the track much faster than I liked, but I dared not touch the brake, even though we were approaching the unsafe bridge. The wild train was right behind us. My heart was in my throat as we reached the bridge, but the train fairly leaped across, and we were soon thundering along the track on the other side, heading toward the first of the switches where Number 19 might be approaching. There

THE PHANTOM TRAIN

was no sign of the train, so I released the brakes, and we shot past the switch in record time.

Suddenly, I saw a red light swinging to and fro on the track in front of us. Was it Number 19 or some other unseen obstacle? Whatever it was, I had to choose quickly between crashing into it or being crashed into by the wild train. In that second, I decided I would rather be run into by a known menace from behind rather than risk smashing into an unknown obstacle in front of us. I reversed the lever and put on the brake. I heard the keen whistle from the wild locomotive blast once, twice, and braced myself for the impact.

Just for a moment, the world went silent. The whistle ceased to wail its warning, and I looked behind me as the wild train leaped forward. Then, just before it reached us, the engine toppled off the track, carrying the whole train down, down into the canyon below. I shuddered, half in relief at our sudden rescue and half in despair for the passengers in the pursuing train. I waited tensely for the cries for help and the terrible hiss of steam, but there was no sound from the black depths below us. All I heard was the rushing of the wind.

The lantern ahead of us had disappeared. I had no choice but to move the train on immediately. This delay may have caused Number 19 to move out along the second switchback, thinking we were already past. We resumed our mad run down the mountain and reached the second switchback just two minutes before Number 19.

I was shaking with shock and relief as I finished the run to Green River. We had traveled so fast that we made record time coming into the station. I was about to climb down from my cab when I saw words forming themselves in the frost on the window. My flesh crawled at the sight. There was no one else in the cab with me and no one outside. Yet the sentences continued to appear before my stricken eyes. The message said: "A freight train was once wrecked in the manner you witnessed this night. The engine was out of control, and four section men were killed. Any man who sees this train and tries to make another run will be wrecked in the same manner as the freight train. You have been warned."

As the last letter finished forming, I jumped out of the cab and went straight into the depot to get a stiff drink and report the wreck I had (or had I?) seen. Later that morning, I resigned from the road and took my family to Denver, where I signed on with the Union Pacific until I retired some years later.

No wreck was ever found in the canyon where I had seen the train crash.

7

The Posthole Digger

SUMMIT COUNTY, UTAH

Ned flung down the shovel and plopped into the dirt, tired, thirsty, and not a little annoyed with his task. He hated fencing! Hated it. But here he was, digging postholes for his grand-daddy. Tomorrow, his granddaddy would sink posts into these holes and string up barbed wire, creating a fence around the pasture where he kept his new mare.

The sun was hot, and Ned was yearning for some water and a bite to eat. Before he could summon up enough energy to go back to the house, his grandmother appeared with a jug of water and a covered dish full of German pastries.

"I thought you would like something to eat, *nicht wahr?*" she said with a smile.

"Yes, ma'am!" Ned said, accepting the plate from her as she shook out her long skirt and took a seat on the ground beside him.

"It is too bad, really, that your granddaddy told the ghost posthole digger to stop. Otherwise, your task would be so much easier," his grandmother said.

Ned sat up straight, his eyes popping.

"A ghost posthole digger?" he shouted.

"Softly, *mein Herz*," his grandmother said. "You will break my ears. *Ja*, we once had a ghost posthole digger come this way."

"When, where, how?" Ned didn't know what to ask first. A ghost! Digging postholes?

His grandmother chuckled. "It was a long time ago now. Your great-grandfather had just moved to Utah. He came from Germany and wished to make a new life in the American Wild West. His Mormon neighbors kindly helped him learn to speak English, though they were disappointed that he did not give up his Protestant roots to become Mormon himself. Your granddaddy went to the local school and soon was speaking English like a native. He was fascinated with the tales of the Comstock Lode in Nevada, the cowboys on the ranges, and the sheep-raising ranches over the border in Wyoming.

"Your granddaddy soon learned the story of the ghost posthole digger. When Senator Warren moved to Wyoming from Massachusetts, he had trouble finding someone to dig postholes for the hundred thousand acres of reserve government land he meant to fence in for his sheep-raising efforts. Later crews would sink posts into these holes, then string the barbed wire up to create the fences he needed for his sheep. Finally, the senator chanced upon an old German man looking for work. The senator hired him immediately, even though the old man spoke not one word of English. The senator's foreman had to use sign language and pantomime to explain to him what the task was. The old German man just kept nodding his gray head and saying "*Ja, ja. Ja, ja.*"

"Finally, the foreman pointed him west, gave him a new shovel, an 8-foot post bar, and a recipe in German for cooking rabbits, and sent him off to work. Soon there was a straight line of new postholes, leading off into the sunset. Two days later, the crews started following the line of holes, putting in new posts and stringing up the barbed wire. But fast as they worked, they never caught up with the German posthole digger. At first, they saw signs of small campfires made along the posthole trail. But eventually these signs faded away, though the postholes still appeared regularly, spaced thirteen paces apart.

"Finally, the crew hit the end of the property they were to fence and turned north. But the postholes did not end with the property. The postholes kept going west, far beyond the property line. No one had bothered to tell the old German man where to stop. The crewmen searched for him but found nothing westward but holes.

"One man rode east, back along the fencing, hoping for some sign that the fellow had turned back. He found the remains of the old man near the ashes of the last campfire. The bones had been stripped clean by vermin. The shovel and post bar were gone, but the German recipe was found clutched in the dead man's hand. The crew could not figure out why the postholes had continued, even after the old man had died. No one could come up with a rational explanation, and no one dared suggest an irrational one.

"Over in Utah, the Mormons began reporting a strange sight. By the light of the full moon, an old man wearing ragged clothes and a long, full gray beard could be seen moving westward and digging, digging, digging postholes with a worn

THE POSTHOLE DIGGER

shovel and a post bar that was the size of a toothpick. During the day, when people would visit the place where the ghost had been seen, they always found a straight line of postholes, thirteen paces apart.

"The children at school used to tease your granddaddy about the ghost, saying that your great-grandfather's property was right in the path of the ghost posthole digger. One lad who lived eastward of your great-grandfather's place said that his father had made him fill in every hole that the ghost had dug on their property after the ghost had passed through their land on the night of the full moon. It had taken him a week to finish the job!

"'The ghost was last seen digging in this area in March,' one young lad told your granddaddy. 'He should be at your house during the next full moon.'

"Your granddaddy asked why the ghost did not stop digging the postholes. The children told him that it was because the ghost did not speak any English, and so he did not know that he had reached the end of the Warren ranch and that his job was done.

"'I can tell him,' your granddaddy said. 'I speak German.'

"So your granddaddy kept a lookout for the German posthole digger. He watched every night for a week, until the seventh night, when there was a full moon. Around midnight, your granddaddy saw a figure appear out in the back pasture. In the moonlight, he could tell it was a small man with a flowing gray beard. He carried a shovel and what seemed to be a small toothpick in his hand. While your granddaddy watched from his window, the man started to dig a hole, right there in the pasture.

"Your granddaddy was so scared of the ghost he could barely move. But he remembered his boast to the other boys at school, and that got him out of bed and down to the yard. He was shivering with fear, but he forced himself to walk over to the old ghost. As he approached, he could hear the ghost singing a German folksong that his mother—your great-grand-mother—used to sing to him when he was small.

"Your granddaddy took heart when he heard the song and walked right up to the ghost.

"'*Guten abend*,' he said, which is German for 'Good evening.'

"The ghost straightened up and gave your granddaddy a huge smile.

"'*Guten abend, guten abend*,' he said happily.

"Your granddaddy asked the ghost what he was doing. The man explained that he had been hired by Senator Warren to dig postholes to the end of his property.

"'Oh,' said your granddaddy, 'but this isn't Senator Warren's ranch. His ranch ended back a piece, up in Wyoming.'

"The ghost was surprised. 'This isn't Senator Warren's ranch?' he asked.

"'No, it is not,' said your granddaddy. 'You are all finished with your work.'

"The ghost leaned against the shovel, thinking hard.

"'All finished,' he said at length. A huge smile lit his face again. 'Then I am to be paid! *Das ist sehr gut.* (That is very good.) *Danke*, my friend. *Danke!*'

"The ghost shook your granddaddy's hand excitedly, then faded away in the moonlight, leaving a line of postholes behind him.

"No one ever saw the ghost posthole digger again. Every once in a while, your granddaddy tries to find out if the ghost ever went back to Senator Warren's ranch to get his pay."

Ned laughed.

"Can you imagine the look on the ranch manager's face if a ghost drifted in and demanded his wages?" he asked.

They both laughed, then his grandmother rose.

"I must get back to the house. Do not forget to come in for lunch."

"I won't," Ned said, standing up and brushing the dirt off his clothes.

He watched his grandmother go back into the house, then picked up his shovel with a sigh. His wished his granddaddy hadn't been so quick to tell the ghost posthole digger that he had reached the end of the Warren property. He wouldn't have minded having a little help putting up this fence.

8

Stampede Mesa

I told Billy it was a bad idea, letting the herd overnight on Stampede Mesa. Oh, I grant you that the grazing atop the 200-acre mesa was nearly always choice. But the history of the place! No one in his right mind would take cattle there, especially if they'd heard the same stories I had.

A cowpoke I know, a real shy fellow named Ted, once told me in confidence that he had seen the ghosts of Stampede Mesa. One stormy evening, while Ted was riding past the mesa, he saw a phantom herd of cattle stampeding in the sky, driven on by a terrible ghost on a blindfolded horse. Then the herd and its guards fell into a cloudy canyon, vanishing before Ted's eyes.

Now, Ted was such a truthful fellow that the other cowpokes called him "Preacher." I believed his story and was real angry when Billy insisted we overnight the herd on Stampede Mesa. But I was outvoted. None of the other cowboys in my outfit would admit to believing in ghosts, and they laughed at me when I suggested we try another place for the night. So I rode a little away from the others, watching my section of

STAMPEDE MESA

cattle and remembering the story of Stampede Mesa and how it came to be haunted.

A fellow named Sawyer started the whole mess in 1889. He was riding the trail with a herd of 1,500 steers. Somewhere along the way about forty head of cows owned by a local homeowner—we call homeowners "nesters"—came trotting into the herd. The nester wasn't far behind, yelling to Sawyer and his men to cut the nester cows out of the herd or else. Well, Sawyer didn't want to be bothered trying to locate a few unbranded nester cows mixed in with the rest. His herd was mighty thin and weary, and he didn't want them prodded about anymore than necessary. When the nester started threatening to stampede the herd if his cows weren't returned to him, Sawyer pulled out his six-shooter and told the nester to get lost.

Sawyer and his outfit got the cattle settled on top of the mesa and were soon snoozing by the fire, except for the night herders, who were watching out for rustlers and such. Well, that nester came back about midnight, mad as a wet hen. He got into the midst of the herd and waved a blanket wildly while he shot off his gun a few times. The herd went mad. The night herders tried to circle the stampeding cattle, but in the end, nearly the whole herd went over the bluff on the south side of the mesa, taking the night herders with them.

Sawyer waited until sunup before sending his men after the nester. They brought him in, horse and all. Sawyer had the nester tied to his horse with a lariat around his neck. They blindfolded the horse and forced the horse and man to back up until they fell off the bluff onto the broken bodies of the dead cattle beneath. Then Sawyer and his men buried their companions and took the remaining 300 head away with them, leaving the nester to rot in the canyon with the cattle.

Ever since that night, the nester's ghost had haunted the mesa, stampeding every herd that dared to rest upon its 200 acres. That's what the other cowpokes said, and I believed them. But Billy didn't believe in ghosts and since Billy was the boss, the men did what he said.

By the time we got the herd settled down for the night, I was real frightened but trying not to show it. I had volunteered to be one of the night herders, and I was jumping at shadows every time one of the cows moved or my partner's saddle creaked.

Round about midnight, my fears came true. A glowing figure appeared out of nowhere, riding toward me. He was waving a blanket and shooting off a gun, though the gun made no sound. The ghost's horse was blindfolded.

To my left, I heard my partner swearing desperately as several steers began stampeding toward the bluffs. I spurred my horse and managed to get in front of them, but the steers passed right through me and my horse, chilling me to the bone. They were phantoms.

The living steers were awake now, bellowing and stamping and ready to run with the phantom herd. I could hear Billy yelling to the other cowhands to saddle up. My partner and I were milling the cattle as best we could, trying to distinguish the real steers from the phantoms. Then I realized that the phantom steers were lighter in color than the living and—there was no other way to describe it—they glowed in the dark. I shouted this information to my partner. Together, we pushed the darker cattle toward one another, using our whips to turn them when they tried to run with the phantoms.

Billy had the whole outfit up and riding within two minutes. We managed to get the real steers huddled together into a restless group while the phantom herd streamed around the perimeter, stampeding over the bluff to the south. It was the hardest thing I ever did, keeping our steers from following the phantoms over that cliff.

About the worst moment for me was when I saw the two phantom night herders swept over the edge with the phantom cattle. I wanted to save them. I started to ride forward as soon as I saw their peril, but Billy yelled frantically at me and I checked myself, realizing there was nothing I could do.

The cattle were frantic for nearly an hour after the last of the phantom herd had passed. It took every man in the outfit to hold them, and they wouldn't settle down for the rest of the night. As soon as it was light enough to travel, Billy got us off that cursed mesa. We lost thirty head that night, but Billy was mighty grateful that it hadn't been the whole herd. He thanked me and my partner again and again for holding the cattle long enough to get the other members of the outfit into the saddle, and he never drove another herd over Stampede Mesa. Once was enough.

9

Pecos Bill and the Haunted House

CARSON CITY, NEVADA

Well now, Pecos Bill was traveling through Nevada when he happened to hear about a frame house just outside Carson City that was supposed to be the most haunted house in the West. Folks about town reckoned that there were nearly two hundred ghosts, spooks, and monsters in that house. Not a single man had stepped foot in it for the last five years. The ghosts and spooks in that haunted house made so much noise howling and shrieking and groaning at night that no one in the neighborhood could get any sleep. Most of the families had already moved away.

Pecos Bill thought it was a cryin' shame that such a nice frame house was going to waste on account of a few spooks, so he volunteered to clear them out for the owner. The owner told Bill he was plumb crazy to consider it.

"But if you can do it, I'll give you my share in the silver mine," said the chap. That suited Bill just fine.

Pecos Bill waited until it was real dark before he went to the haunted house. He wanted to make sure all the ghosts were present so he could clean up the whole house in one go. As he waited for the ghosts to come out, Bill filled his six-shooter with silver bullets, 'cause everyone in the West knows that werewolves can only be killed by silver bullets.

The full moon peeped over the horizon. Inside the house, several ghosts started a-moaning and a-groaning. A banshee rose right up through the roof and howled dramatically as it waved its arms about. Bill watched the banshee swoop out over the roof and fly right through the front door.

Around the side of the house, the ground split open, and a group of skeletons came clattering out onto the grass. They rattled and shook their way into the house, climbing in a window that a mummy held open.

The howling and shrieking and groaning from the house was deafening. Pecos Bill decided that most of the ghosts and spooks and monsters were out and about by now, so he sauntered up the walk and opened the front door.

As soon as Pecos Bill entered the front hallway, the air was filled with a loud "Ooooooo." A banshee flew straight at Bill, its red eyes burning, claws extended. Bill stepped aside at the last minute, and the banshee sailed right past him and got caught halfway through a tree. One down, one hundred and ninety-nine to go, Bill reckoned.

Something groaned in the corner of the entryway. A mummy emerged, arms outstretched, reaching for Pecos Bill. Bill grabbed hold of a loose bandage and whirled the mummy around so fast it became unwrapped and retreated back to its corner in embarrassment.

A pack of werewolves came running down from the second floor, determined to swallow Pecos Bill. But Bill was the fastest shot in the West. He pulled out his six-shooter and shot all six werewolves lickety-split.

Several dozen banshees had followed the werewolves down the steps. Bill bashed their heads together and threw them out the front door after the first banshee. Then he ambled into the front room and sweet-talked ten hags into turning respectable.

There came a long, unearthly howl from the back room. A giant demon hound with one flaming red eye raced toward Bill. Bill jumped right on its back, and the hound bucked and twisted even worse than Bill's horse Widow Maker on a bad day. But Bill had once ridden a tornado, so a demon hound, even one the size of an elephant, posed no problems for him. Finally, the hound collapsed to the floor and lay at Bill's feet, wagging its giant tail.

Pecos Bill was getting bored. There just wasn't enough of a challenge for him, taking on the spooks a few at a time. So Bill got out his lasso, and he roped a hundred of them ghosts all at once. He dragged them down the street to the cemetery and forced them back into the grave.

Returning to the frame house, Pecos Bill found the skeletons dancing in the kitchen. He decided to join in, and waltzed them around and around so fast that they broke apart.

A couple dozen zombies tried to chase Pecos Bill out of the house, but Bill just stood at the top of the stairs and knocked them down one by one until they lay in a heap in the hallway. Then Bill picked the zombies up, took them outside, and reburied them. That left just the toughest spooks and monsters in the frame house.

PECOS BILL AND THE HAUNTED HOUSE

The largest of the monsters and the leader of the pack was a huge creature with fourteen eyes and about twenty tentacles. The monster came rolling up to Bill, and the two of them wrestled up and down and around the house until sunrise. Finally, Bill got the creature's tentacles tied behind its back. Using the tentacles as a sling, Bill shot the creature right up to the moon, where it still haunts the dark side to this day.

As soon as the other monsters saw what happened to their leader, they were so scared that they raced out of every door and window of the haunted house. When they were gone, Bill carefully checked every corner. He ran out two small ghosts that were lurking up the chimney. Then he brought in the local priest to bless the house and presented it to its owner.

The owner was so happy he gave Pecos Bill his share in the Ophir mine, the richest mine in the Comstock Lode. The families in the neighborhood threw him the biggest ball ever held in Carson City.

Not one of the ghosts ever came back to that haunted house. Guess they were too scared of what Pecos Bill might do to them if they returned.

10

La Llorona

Anita's son lay tossing and turning on the narrow bed. The doctor—who was also her brother, Manuel—brushed cool water
over his young nephew's forehead, his face grave. He looked up
and urged Anita to lie down and rest, but she couldn't.

Instead, Anita nursed the baby and laid her down in her
cradle to sleep. Then she stumbled out of the adobe house
into the still, dark night, seeking solace in her favorite place
near the river. It was her fault, Anita thought numbly, sitting
down on the ground near the soft swish of the water. She had
sent her son to play with the children from town, forgetting
the report of fever that had reached her the week before.
She had been numb with fatigue, having stayed up all night
with the baby, who had colic. Anita had given in to her
son's pleading without thinking. Now he lay dying, and it
was all her fault.

Manuel did not say anything, but she knew that he held
little hope for her son. He had told her to send a message to
her husband, who was away on business. She had done so,
not knowing what to say. Finally she had written: "Come

immediately. Our son is ill." She knew her husband would leave at once, for he dearly loved his son.

Anita folded her arms around her raised knees and shivered though the night was not cold. Her husband would never forgive her if his son died because of her carelessness. She would never forgive herself. Anita moaned in anguish and buried her face in her arms.

Across the river, an answering wail echoed the terrible guilt and pain she felt. Anita's skin turned to ice. Slowly, she looked up. Floating just above the water near the edge of the river was the white figure of a woman. The woman wrung her hands in agony and gave another heart-wrenching wail.

Anita sat frozen in fear, gazing at the ghost. It was La Llorona. The Wailing Woman.

"*Madre de Dios,*" she whispered, clutching at the cross she always wore around her neck.

She remembered all the stories she had heard about La Llorona. One story said that La Llorona had been a widow who wished to marry a rich nobleman. The nobleman did not want to raise another man's children, and he dismissed her. So the widow had drowned her children to be free of them. When she told the nobleman what she had done, he was horrified and would have nothing more to do with her. As she left him, the widow was overcome by the terrible crime she had committed and went to the river, looking for her children. But they were gone. She drowned herself, but her spirit was condemned to wander the waterways, weeping and searching for her children until the end of time.

LA LLORONA

Another version of the story told of a man who was married to a beautiful woman. The man was too poor to raise a child, so after the birth of his first son, he drowned the child in the river while his wife, too weak from the birth to stop him, pleaded in vain with him to spare the child. Several more sons were born, and the man drowned every one. When the poor man took the last baby boy to the river, his wife followed even though she was still weak and bleeding from giving birth. When he threw the child in the river, the woman went in after him, determined to save the boy even though she did not know how to swim. The woman and her son both drowned. But the woman's spirit came back, haunting the river and its banks, crying out for her lost children. The sound drove her husband mad. Finally, he grabbed a knife and jumped into the river after the spirit to kill her, and he drowned as well. The spirit of the woman still haunts the waters, weeping and wailing and searching for her sons.

Both of these tales sped through Anita's mind as the white figure of La Llorona moved slowly toward land, toward where she was sitting on the riverbank. Anita could almost make out the beautiful face of the ghost, made terrible by the grief that kept her haunting the river ways. The ghost was weeping and wringing her hands as she paused at the edge of the river.

All the pain and guilt Anita felt over the illness of her own small son overwhelmed her suddenly, and she and La Llorona wept out their grief together. Anita wondered, even as she wept, if it was her pain that had drawn the ghost to her that night.

Anita never knew how long she sat weeping by the river. It might have been hours, or just a few moments. Suddenly, a light streamed out from the door to the house, and she heard her brother call her name. She stood, her legs tingling with numbness, and turned toward the sound. Her heart beat rapidly in fear. Was it the end already? Her husband had not yet arrived. Please, *Dios,* please let it not be the end!

Manuel hurried toward her and caught her up into a big hug. "The fever has broken," he cried ecstatically. "He will live!"

If Manuel had not been holding her, Anita would have fallen to the ground with relief. From somewhere by the river, she heard the sound of weeping growing fainter and fainter. Anita glanced back, but her eyes were dazzled by the light streaming from the doorway and she could not see La Llorona. She knew that the wailing woman was leaving the riverbank, leaving Anita to rejoice in her living son, while the ghost continued to weep and to search for the sons she had lost.

11

The House of the Candle

CASTROVILLE, TEXAS

After spending many years in the army as a hospital steward, I decided to retire. I purchased a small house in Castroville and settled down to enjoy my leisure. Castroville was just a tiny town back then, with a couple of churches, a convent, and a small trading post where you could hear all the local gossip. I had a garden to putter in, a couple of buddies who liked to play checkers during the evening, a nice dog, and some chickens. It was a good life.

Of course, once the folks in town discovered I had worked as a hospital steward, they started coming to me for medical assistance, since Castroville didn't have a doctor. That kept me very busy. I was called out for everything from pneumonia to spotty rashes. It was a good thing I had inherited my mother's iron constitution or I would have died a long time ago, breathing in all that bad air and disease. Mama always said that the only way a Dawson could be killed was to hit them over the head with a hammer, and I was living proof of that.

There was one fellow in town who never seemed to get sick. His name was Auguste Gauchemain. A Frenchman, he had settled in Castroville about ten years ago. Auguste spent most of his time digging in his garden and minding his own business. He never spoke of his past, but the townsfolk liked to speculate about Auguste, wondering how the good-looking Frenchman came to have a scarred right hand and why he was so afraid of the dark. This fear was the kind you expected to see in a young child. Auguste always carried a lantern with him, even in the daytime, just in case he was caught out after dark. At home, he always kept the house lit with candles from dusk to dawn. If he were going out for the evening, he would light several candles, so he wouldn't come home to a dark house.

People used to tease Auguste about his fondness for the light. Harry, the man who ran the trading post, once asked him why he wasted so much money on candles. Auguste told him that he had fallen once and badly scarred his hand. Ever since then, he refused to walk in the dark. I was rather skeptical of this explanation. Auguste's fear was too strong to be caused by a fall, even one that resulted in an injury.

In spite of his intensely private nature, Auguste loved company. He would visit the trading post almost every night and watch the old men playing checkers. He would attend evening services at both churches and was always seeking out someone to walk him home after dark.

One day, Auguste stopped beside my front fence to ask me to take a look at some insects that had gotten into his garden. I followed him to his small house, and we got to talking about this and that as I inspected his plants. I gave him directions on how to control the pests and asked him if he ever played checkers. Auguste said he liked to watch but admitted that he did not understand the game. So I brought over my checker-board that evening and taught him how to play.

I had never been inside Auguste's house before. It was small—just one room—and all the nooks and crannies were stuffed with candles. It was brighter than noontime inside that house. Auguste bought extra large candles, the kind usually used in churches. The owner of the trading post had told everyone in town that Auguste bought them by the gross and always paid cash. Seeing how many Auguste lit that night, I believed it.

After that, Auguste would sometimes play checkers with us at the trading post. We would have tournaments, and Auguste got to be pretty good. Not as good as me, but I had the advantage of playing checkers with the best the army had to offer for more years than I care to remember.

I noticed one evening that Auguste was looking feverish and had a cough. When I questioned him, he admitted that he wasn't feeling well, and he left the game early. I told him I would drop by later that night to give him a dose of patent medicine. Auguste thanked me and went home to his bright house, carrying his lantern.

The game went a little late, so it was nearly midnight when I reached Auguste's house. I was startled to see that only one candle was burning. Auguste must really be feeling ill if he hadn't taken time to light all his candles. I knocked on the door and went in when he called to me. I fussed about, giving Auguste a large dose of patent medicine and plumping up the pillows so he felt comfortable. He was pale, and his hands were trembling. I was worried about him, though I kept my manner

The House of the Candle

jolly. The first thing I learned as a hospital steward was the importance of keeping up a patient's spirits.

We sat talking for about half an hour. Then a clap of thunder burst overhead, and I realized that a storm was rolling in. I jumped up and grabbed my hat.

"I will stop by tomorrow evening to check on you," I told Auguste. "You should rest all day tomorrow. Don't get up."

I clapped my hat on my head and opened the door. The wind was gusting fiercely as I hurried out. The candle flickered and then went out as I closed the door. At once, Auguste gave a terrible cry. I was astonished.

"Auguste, what's wrong?" I shouted through the door.

"My light, it has gone out!" Auguste called out in a panic.

"You'll sleep better without it," I shouted back.

"*Non, non!*" Auguste cried desperately. "*S'il vous plaît,* light my candle."

I didn't understand why he was so frightened of the darkness, but I went back into the house and groped around for the tinderbox. I could hear Auguste's teeth chattering. His fever must be rising, I thought to myself.

"Hurry! Hurry, *mon ami!*" Auguste whispered, his voice shaking with fear. "I cannot endure it much longer. *Regardez!* He draws near to kill me! Go away! Go away!"

I was startled and a little frightened when I heard his words. My hand was shaking as I lit the candle, and I quickly looked around the small room. There was no one there. I looked at Auguste. He was as white as a ghost and covered with sweat. His whole body trembled in terror. I pulled out my flask of brandy and pressed it to his shaking lips. After taking a long drink, Auguste fell back onto the pillows and looked up at me in mute thankfulness.

I wondered if the fever had caused this trembling, or if it were something else entirely. Overhead, the rain started to pound on the roof of the house, and the thunder clapped again. I felt his forehead to see if the fever had gotten worse.

"It is not the sickness that bothers me," said Auguste quietly, wringing his shaking hands. "It is my conscience. I would rejoice, *mon ami,* if this sickness took my life, for then I would be free at last."

I sat silently. I didn't know what to say. He continued, "I know you will not betray me while I live, so I will tell you my story. Back in my country, I was engaged to a beautiful girl. Oh, *mon ami,* I was so much in love with her. But she betrayed me with another. *Oui,* I found them together, and the man and I exchanged bitter words. He pulled a knife on me and slashed at my hand, giving me the scars you see upon it. In my pain and jealousy, I grabbed the knife from him and stabbed him in the heart. My beautiful girl, she screamed and sobbed and flung herself down beside her lover. I knew I had to flee at once or be sent to prison. I grabbed money and a few possessions from my house and went to the seaport. There was a ship leaving for Mexico, and I took a place on board as a sailor. From Mexico, I came north to Texas, and settled here in Castroville.

"I thought I was safe here. Then I started dreaming of my enemy each night. It is always the same dream. My enemy is drenched in his own blood and is coming to kill me. He carries the same knife he used to slash my hand, and I know he has come to cut out my heart. I discovered that if I kept the candles burning all night, then my enemy would not appear in my dreams. But for the last few weeks, I have seen my enemy during the day. I do not know what to do. I burn the candles all the time now, day and night. And still he comes!"

I spoke soothingly to Auguste, troubled by his story but not willing to show my concern to my patient. By the time the storm had passed, Auguste was in a much better frame of mind. He fell asleep, and I stood for a moment watching the candlelight flicker across his face. It was hard to think of him as a killer. He did not seem the type who would harm any man.

After returning home that night, I was called to a birth outside town and didn't get to Auguste's house until after nine o'clock the next evening. I knew at once that something was wrong. The house was dark and silent as I approached. I knocked, but there was no answer. Fearing the worst, I entered the house and struck a light.

Auguste lay on the bed, his face twisted in terror, his hands clasped to his heart, as if clutching an invisible knife. The candle beside his bed had guttered out. He was dead.

The Sandstorm

"Hey Charlie!"

I heard Drew shouting from somewhere behind me and turned in the saddle to look over my shoulder. Drew and I had been working cattle together for years, and I knew him better than I knew my brother. When Drew spoke in that tone, there was trouble coming. He had halted his horse and was looking around apprehensively.

"What's the matter?" I called, stopping my horse.

"I think a sandstorm is coming," Drew said. "The wind is picking up, and the air feels funny."

I didn't like the sound of this. Drew's weather predictions were nearly always right. We were riding homeward along the Diablo Trail and were too far from the ranch to reach it before the storm hit.

"We'd better camp out near those rocks, then," I said. "They should provide some shelter."

Drew agreed, and we hurriedly rigged up a shelter and tethered the horses. I could hear the storm approaching as we crawled into our rough shelter with our supplies and the canteens. There was not much water left and very little food. If the storm lasted longer than a day, we would be in trouble.

Then the storm hit, blasting hot sand into my eyes, my hair, and my skin. The wind whirled above, around, and under our shelter, which offered no protection at all. Even the rocks did little to shield us from the terrible pounding and the heat. We took small sips of water every hour or so to relieve the dryness of our throats. It was also necessary to shift about to keep from being buried completely under the sand. It was so hard to breathe that I thought I would suffocate in that howling sandstorm. I lay on my side, trying to breathe through my sleeve as much as I could, to keep the sand out of my nose. Every once in a while I would check to make sure Drew was all right.

A day passed in these terrible conditions. We drank the last of our water and ate the last of our food, and still the wind and sand whipped about us in an impenetrable curtain as the heat dried out our bodies. One after the other our horses dropped dead and were gradually buried under the sand. My tongue was swollen, and I couldn't part my lips. My throat was so dry it felt like sandpaper, and all I could think about, when I thought at all, was water.

Beside me, Drew hadn't moved in over an hour. I nudged him, shaking the sand away, trying to rouse him. After a very long time, he opened his eyes a slit, so I knew he was still alive.

Another hour had passed when I noticed that the sound of the storm was muted, though there was no decrease in the pounding of the wind and the sand. Through the whipping sand rode a man dressed all in white. His hat was of white

The Sandstorm

cowhide, his shirt the finest linen, and he was riding a beautiful pure white horse. He was followed by eleven riders, who were also dressed in white. Their spurs, bits, and stirrups gleamed of silver; their belt buckles were gold. They were leading a white horse behind them. I tried to call out to them, but my lips were swollen shut, and I made no sound.

They must have seen us, because the procession stopped in front of our half-buried figures, and two men dismounted. They walked over to Drew and picked him up. Tenderly, they helped him over to the riderless horse and helped him mount. I was waiting for them to return for me, but instead they mounted their horses. Drew was motioned to take the place behind the leader, then the men in white started riding away. I pried my lips apart with my fingers and gave a hoarse cry of protest. But they kept riding away, leaving me alone in the storm.

They disappeared into the distance, one by one. All save the last rider, who paused and turned his horse back toward me. My heart leaped in relief. But he stopped after only a few yards and called out, "Be patient, Charlie. It is not your time yet. We will come back for you one day." Then he passed out of sight, and I was alone. I laid my head down on my arms. I would have wept, but I had no water left in me. Slowly, the world grew dark, and I knew no more.

I was awakened by someone shaking my shoulder. I opened my eyes and looked into the face of Doc Ramsey, the physician from town. I realized that I was lying on my bed in the bunkhouse, and that my bunkmates were gathered in a semicircle behind the doctor, who was holding a cup with vile-tasting medicine to my lips. I drank, coughed, and drank again.

"Well, Charlie, you are one lucky fellow. Most men wouldn't have lived through a storm like that," said Doc Ramsey.

"What about Drew?" I asked, struggling to sit up. Doc Ramsey pushed me back down against the pillow. "Did the white riders bring him home?"

My bunkmates exchanged sober glances. Doc Ramsey took a deep breath and said, "Drew didn't make it, Charlie. I'm sorry. He was already dead when we found you."

I realized then why the white riders had left me behind. It was not my time, the last rider had said.

Doc Ramsey chased everyone out of the bunkhouse and left me alone to rest. Just before sleep claimed me, I recalled the final words of the white rider: "We will come back for you one day," he had said. So I knew I would see Drew again.

13

The Lonely Caballero

SANTA FE, NEW MEXICO

There was once a lonely caballero named Diego who was serving with a regiment here in Sante Fe. He was a handsome devil and popular with the other soldiers. But the ladies thought him haughty and cold, and he could find no señorita to attend the dances with him.

They had fine dances in those days, one each month. The men of the regiment took turns hosting the dances, each man with a beautiful señorita to act as his hostess. But Diego had no lady to stand on the receiving line with him and to dance the opening dance. He felt ashamed when he thought of the dance he was to host that month, all alone. How the men in his regiment would laugh! Diego's pride would not allow that.

So Diego started searching for a lady to act as his hostess. All of the women he knew turned him down flat, and he dared not ask any of the señoritas who were being courted by the men in his regiment. Then one day Diego saw a beautiful woman having coffee in the plaza. She would make a fine hostess, he thought, and so he offered to refill her cup from the pot left on the table for her. The lady smiled politely as he performed this service but would not speak to him, though he lingered at her table for a good while.

Still, Diego was persistent. Every day he would go to the plaza to see if the señorita was there. If she was, he would refill her coffee cup and try to strike up a conversation. One day, Diego stole her handkerchief when she was looking the other way. That night, he presented himself at her house to return it. The servant turned him away.

The next time Diego saw the beautiful lady, he chided her for having him turned away from her house. He was only trying to return her handkerchief, he claimed. Diego's words displeased her. "I have lost no handkerchief," she said. She went away in a temper, and Diego knew that he had ruined his chance with her.

Diego was desperate now. The dance was only three days away, and he had no hostess. He would look like a fool in front of his regiment! Diego decided to put a love charm on the beautiful señorita, and he went in search of a soldier who had grown up in Sante Fe. The man told Diego of two witches who lived near the plaza who might help him solve his problem. Diego thanked him and hurried to the proper address.

Diego knocked on the witches' door, and a wrinkled old woman answered his knock. He explained his mission, but his manner was so cold and haughty that the woman took offense and tried to shut the door in his face. Diego caught the door in a strong grip to keep it open, and he begged her to help him. When she thought him sufficiently humbled, she let Diego in.

A second, younger woman was stirring a cauldron in the corner. She ignored Diego, and after a startled glance at the glowing pot, he turned back to the old woman. She would give him nothing until she had seen his money. Diego took the coins from his pocket and counted them out for her.

"You have seen my money," said Diego, "now give me a love potion." The young woman in the corner laughed when she heard his words. Diego turned to glare at her. She looked him in the eye and said: "In love, as in life, there are no guarantees. Save your money, and mend your attitude. This will help you more than any love potion."

Diego was angered by her words. He turned away and insisted that the old woman give him a love potion. The old woman took the coins from him and handed him a vial filled with green liquid. Diego marched away, vowing never to go near the witches again.

Diego went down the street to the plaza and saw the beautiful señorita sitting at her favorite table, drinking coffee. Although annoyed at his presence, good manners forbade her from refusing his offer to pour her more coffee. As he picked up the pot, Diego took her handkerchief from his pocket. He flourished it in front of her, and she snatched it from him. While she tucked it away, Diego poured the potion into her coffee and handed her the cup. She drank it as fast as she could and hastened away from the table.

Diego was not sure how long it would take for the potion to work, so he waited a whole day before going to the señorita's house to ask her to be his hostess at the dance. The servant who opened the door refused him entry, saying his mistress never wanted to see him again. Furious, Diego pushed the man aside and went into the house.

The señorita was angry when she saw him. She told Diego in no uncertain terms that she wanted nothing further to do with him and had him thrown from the house. Furious and humiliated, Diego ran to the house where the witches lived. He burst through the front door uninvited and threatened the wrinkled old woman with his sword.

"You are a fraud! Give me my money back," he said to the old woman.

"Return my vial, and I will return your money," she replied calmly, unafraid of his sword. Diego took the vial from his pocket and thrust it at her. The old woman shook her head.

"This vial is empty," she said. "I cannot accept it."

Diego was shaking with rage. "Give me my money, or I will slit your throat," he threatened, pointing the tip of the sword at her neck.

The young woman came through a door in the back of the room. When she saw Diego, she said, "I told you that there were no guarantees in love. If the señorita has already given her heart to another, the potion will not work."

Diego glared at her, grabbed the old woman, and held the sword against her throat. "Give me my money, or this old woman dies."

The young woman spoke a single, magic word, and a long knife appeared out of thin air. She gave a small nod, and the knife flew straight at Diego and cut off his head. Diego's head rolled out the door and down the street—thumpity, thumpity, thump—and landed next to the table in the plaza where the señorita liked to drink her coffee.

THE LONELY CABALLERO

From that day to this, the spirit of the lonely caballero rides back and forth along the river, searching for his head. If anyone dares to approach him, he threatens them with his sword, as he once threatened a wrinkled old woman. He never finds his head, though it can be heard on dark nights, thumping its way down the street and into the plaza.

14

Lafitte's Ghost

LAPORTE, TEXAS

It was the worst sort of blustery night, and I wanted to get in out of the rain almost as much as my poor horse, who was dripping and snorting and shaking his mane every few yards to emphasize his displeasure. I was eager to get home, for I had not seen my wife since the war with the North broke out. I had a two-year-old son whom I had never met. But I knew it was best to get in out of the rain and finish the trip tomorrow. I was not too far from LaPorte, and I decided to ask the first homeowner I saw if I could bunk down in the stable.

I immediately started looking for a dwelling, but it was nearly an hour before I saw an old house looming through the driving rain. I rode right up to the stable and took my horse in. The stable was vacant and looked as if it had been that way for many years. I made my horse as comfortable as I could and hurried through the rain to the house, carrying my saddle and blanket. The front door was barred, and the house had an air of vacancy and neglect about it. I shouted and knocked, but no one answered. Lugging my saddle and blanket with me, I went around the side of the house, trying windows until I found one that was open. I shoved my gear inside and climbed in after it.

Removing and lighting a match from an inner pocket, I was surprised to see a nice room with a stack of wood right beside the fireplace. I made my way through the darkness to the fireplace, lit another match, and made a fire. Once the chill had faded from the room, I made myself comfortable on the floor, using the saddle as a pillow and covering myself with the blanket. I was asleep at once and dreamed happily of my wife and son.

Then my dream changed, and I was watching the devil building a castle on Galveston Island. I recognized it immediately. It was the home of Jean Lafitte, the Pirate of the Gulf. He had promised the devil the life and soul of the first creature he cast eyes upon in payment for the castle and arranged to have a dog thrown into his tent at sunrise. So the devil received a dog instead of a human soul. I chuckled to myself, and the devil must have heard me, for he turned and looked straight at me. His gaze was cold, and it turned me to ice.

I awoke, shaking, and saw the figure of a man looming over me in the firelight. He stood impossibly still, and I could discern no breath coming from him. I blinked in surprise and fear when I realized that he was glowing and I could see the wall through his body.

"*Viens avec moi,*" the ghost said. "Come with me! You must free me."

"Who are you?" I asked, amazed at the steadiness of my voice. I wanted to run away, but I was too scared to move a muscle.

"I am Jean Lafitte," the ghost wailed. The sound made my skin crawl. "I have been condemned to roam the earth

LAFITTE'S GHOST

until a worthy soul finds my ill-gotten treasure and uses it to feed the poor, help the sick, and do other acts of goodness. *Viens avec moi.*"

"I would love to help, but I have to go home to my wife and child," I said. "Good night." I stuck my head under the blanket and pretended to go back to sleep. The ghost gave a threatening wail, but I kept my head covered. My heart was pounding so loud I was sure the ghost could hear it.

I was not interested in a treasure that would not benefit myself or my family. As a church-going man, I appreciated the concept of charity, but I firmly believed that charity begins at home. Besides, I had no idea if the ghost was telling the truth. When I peeped out from under the blanket, the ghost was gone.

A gust of wind drove the rain against the window, and I moved closer to the fire and put on more wood. I was trying to decide if I should go outside and be wet and miserable or stay inside and be dry and terrified. Another fierce burst of rain decided me. Definitely dry and terrified.

It took me quite a while to get back to sleep. I finally dozed off and dreamed that I was a privateer serving under Lafitte on Galveston Island. At his command, I would help smuggle slaves and merchandise past the customs inspectors. Lafitte was not a bad chief, except when someone disobeyed. He had one man hanged because he dared to attack a ship against orders. The privateers gathered around the fire at night and told Lafitte stories to me since I was a newcomer to the business. Their favorite story was about Governor William C. Caliborne of Louisiana, who dared to offer a $500 reward for the arrest and delivery of Lafitte. Lafitte retaliated by offering $5,000 for the arrest and delivery of Governor Caliborne. The governor was enraged and sent out an expedition to seize Lafitte, but Lafitte's men ambushed the expedition and sent them back to New Orleans, loaded with presents. The privateers all laughed uproariously at this story, and I laughed with them. Then Lafitte appeared and gave me a glare that chilled me to the bone.

I awoke, shaking. I knew at once that I was not alone. The ghost of Lafitte was staring down at me. "*Viens avec moi!*" he commanded. "You will come with me right now." He reached down and picked me up. Where his hands touched me, my skin turned ice cold, and I gasped. The ghost beckoned me to follow him and went out into the hall. I hesitated for a moment, but when Lafitte frowned, I followed, not wanting him to touch me again. Lafitte stopped at the third door and glided through it. I started tiptoeing back to the fire, but Lafitte stuck his ghostly head through the heavy wood of the door and glared at me. I tiptoed back and entered the room in the normal fashion. Lafitte's ghost stood at the center of the floor.

"Behold," the Pirate of the Gulf said grandly. The floor became transparent, and I could see mounds of gold, silver, and jewels buried deep beneath the house. "This treasure cost me my soul," said the ghost. "You must give it to the poor so I can be free. You must help me!"

He was glaring at me again, and my skin crawled in sheer terror. The room was as icy as the grave, and Lafitte's ghost grew larger and more menacing the longer I hesitated. The gold was tempting, but I knew that if I took it I would keep it, rather than offering it to the poor. Then Lafitte's ghost would start to haunt my house in revenge. I did not think my wife would approve of that.

"You've got the wrong fellow," I gasped, backing away from the glowing figure of Lafitte. Lafitte gave a shout of rage and reached toward me, his arms growing longer and longer. Outside, the rain was still driving down, and the wind was howling fiercely, but I decided I would rather be wet and miserable than dry and dead. I ran back to my room, grabbed my saddle and blanket, and vaulted out the window.

My horse was none too happy when I saddled him up and rode him out into the storm, but I was surely not going to stay on that property. As I rode away, a great howl rose up from the house. I could hear the ghost's voice wailing, "Help me! Help me!"

"Help yourself," I shouted back. I rode the rest of the way home without stopping and spent the next night in my wife's arms.

15

The Lantern

YUMA, ARIZONA

When me and my pal Eddie met up in Yuma a few years back, we got talking about lost mines and that mother lode of gold we both knew was still out there somewhere in the desert. Eddie was obsessed with finding Pegleg Smith's lost gold— black ore sprinkled through and through with yellow nuggets of pure gold, just waiting for someone to come by and pick it up. Me, I didn't much care where we prospected, just so long as we ended up finding gold. Finding lots of gold was an essential part of my future plans, plans that included a mansion on easy street and a buxom lass named Bess, whom I had decided to make Missus Matthew Kelly, if I got up the nerve to ask her. I was tired of being a poor blacksmith. Bess deserved a rich man, and that was what I was aiming to be.

Eddie rustled up a couple of burros, and we hightailed it into the desert, looking for old Pegleg's three buttes, one of which was covered with burned, black ore full of gold. We were trying to figure out the shortcut Pegleg took from Yuma to Los Angeles, but we got turned around somehow, examining all the buttes we came across for gold. I didn't know there were so many gol-durned buttes out there! We wandered around for days and days, until our supplies started getting kind of low. Finally, I put my foot down.

"Eddie, ol' pal," I said firmly, "I am aiming to get rich out here, not dead. Our supplies are getting mighty low, and we are in the middle of nowhere. The fact is, we are so far off track that we're closer to Vallecito station than we are to Los Angeles. Me and my burro, we are heading to Vallecito station. You can go where you want."

I set off in the direction I thought led toward Vallecito station, hoping that I would get my bearings once we got a bit closer. I soon heard Eddie coming along behind me, grumbling about how pig-headed and stubborn I was. I didn't care what Eddie said. I wasn't planning on being dead. No sir! Being dead would be terribly inconvenient to my future plans.

Well, by nightfall we had covered a lot of hot, prickly desert, and I had my bearings at last. It wouldn't be long before we reached the station. I settled down between a rock and a hard place for the night, with my back toward the fire. The stars were shining brightly overhead, and I got to dreaming about my big mansion and the black-eyed Bess whom I planned to ask to share it with me.

Bess was just about to give me a kiss when I was rudely awakened by a shout in my ear. I looked up into Eddie's ugly mug and almost slugged him. But he was pretty panic-stricken about something, so I hauled myself up and looked around. The burros were making a racket just beyond the firelight, and Eddie was clutching his rifle and babbling away about a skeleton.

I figured Eddie'd had a bad dream and I had just decided to give him a thrashing for waking me up, when I saw the light.

At first, I thought it was reflected firelight. But the light was flickering oddly and seemed to bounce up and down. I grabbed my rifle and walked away from the fire toward what turned out to be a lantern— a lantern suspended within the chest cavity of a huge skeleton. From the aimless, stumbling way it was walking, the light from the lantern wasn't doing the skeleton much good.

I'd never admit it to Eddie, but the sight of that 8-foot-tall skeleton made my flesh creep. I told myself it was just Eddie playing tricks on me 'cause he was mad about our change in destination. To prove it, I took aim at the ghastly creature and fired off a couple of shots. The shots didn't faze the skeleton at all. In fact, my shots didn't even make the lantern flicker. That scared me. I knew then that this was no trick. It was some kind of terrible phantom, stalking the desert at night.

Repelled and fascinated, I followed the skeleton for several minutes, watching it stoop occasionally toward the ground as if it was looking for something. Then it kept going. Eddie wasn't far behind me, though he didn't say a word. The odd, stumbling gait of the skeleton made me think somehow of Pegleg Smith. Old Pegleg might have walked like that once, and maybe he still did. The skeleton entered a valley, and I lost sight of it. By that time, I'd had enough of this supernatural encounter. I returned to our camp and soon was sleeping between that rock and a hard place. Eddie didn't say anything; he just lay back down next to the fire and stayed there until morning.

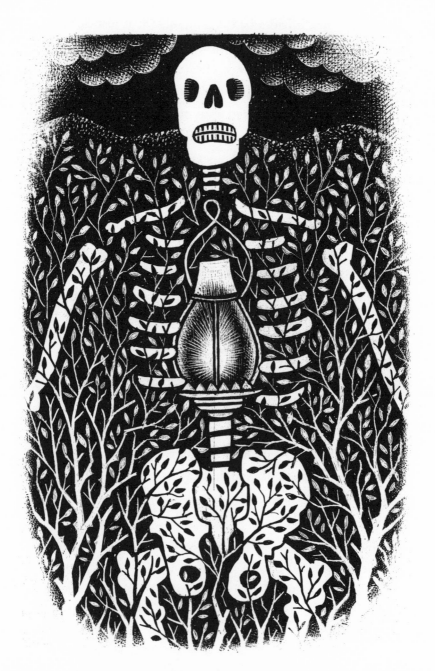

THE LANTERN

As soon as we got to Vallecito station, Eddie took the next stage out of there, not caring where it went. The last I heard of Eddie, he was working as a clerk in Phoenix. I guess the walking skeleton got to him somehow. Me, I went back to Yuma and proposed to Bess. I'd given up my big dreams. My mansion turned out to be a small adobe house, and my fortune—such as it was—was made as a blacksmith rather than a miner. Still, it was a better future than being dead—or haunting in the desert with a lantern in my chest! And I got my Bess, which was the best part of the whole adventure.

PART TWO
Powers of Darkness and Light

16

The Dance

Lacey hurried through her schoolwork as fast as she could. It was the night of the Kingsville high school dance, and Lacey couldn't wait until seven o'clock, the time the dance was to begin. She had purchased a brand-new, sparkly red dress for the occasion. She knew she looked smashing in it. It was going to be the best evening of her life.

Then her mother came in the house, looking pale and determined.

"Lacey, I need to speak with you," her mother said.

Lacey looked up from her books. "What is it, Mama?"

"You are not going to that dance," her mother said.

Lacey was shocked. Not go to the dance? That was ridiculous! All her friends were going. She had bought an expensive new dress just for this occasion.

"But why?" Lacey asked her mother.

"I've just been talking to the preacher. He says the dance is going to be for the devil. You are absolutely forbidden to go," her mother said.

Lacey argued and protested, but her mother remained firm.

She would not let Lacey attend the dance. Finally, Lacey nodded as if she accepted her mother's words. But she was determined to go to the dance. As soon as her mother was busy cleaning the kitchen, she put on her brand-new red dress and ran down to the hall where the dance was being held.

As soon as Lacey walked into the room, all the boys turned to look at her. She was startled by all the attention. Normally, no one noticed her. Her mother sometimes accused her of being too awkward to get a boyfriend. But she was not awkward that night. The boys in her class were fighting with each other to dance with her. The other girls watched her with envy. Even her best friend snubbed her. But Lacey didn't care—she was popular at last, and she was going to make the most of it.

Later, Lacey broke away from the crowd and went to the table to get some punch to drink. She heard a sudden hush. The music stopped. When she turned, she saw a handsome man with jet-black hair and clothes standing next to her.

"Dance with me," he said.

Lacey managed to stammer a "yes," completely stunned by this gorgeous man. The man led her out on the dance floor. The music sprang up at once. She found herself dancing better than she had ever danced before. Slowly everyone else stopped dancing to watch them. Lacey was elated. They were the center of attention.

Then the man spun Lacey around and around. She gasped for breath, trying to step out of the spin. But her partner spun her faster and faster, until her feet felt hot and the floor seemed to melt under her. Lacey's eyes fixed in horror on the man's

The Dance

face as he twirled her even faster. She saw his eyes burning with red fire, as he gave her a smile of pure evil. For the first time, she noticed two horns protruding from his forehead. Lacey gasped desperately for breath, terrified because she now knew with whom she was dancing.

The man in black spun Lacey so fast that a cloud of dust flew up around them both, hiding them from the crowd. When the dust settled, Lacey was gone. The man in black bowed once to the assembled students and teachers, then vanished. The devil had come to the party, and he had spun Lacey all the way to hell.

17

The Bear Lake Monster

BEAR LAKE, UTAH

"Janie, I'm going out hunting," Abe yelled over his shoulder, grabbing his rifle and stalking out the front door. He was annoyed and didn't bother to hide it. The curtain at the kitchen window twitched, and he saw Jane peer out at him anxiously. She knew that Abe only went hunting when he was upset about something. She probably thought he was upset at her. Normally, Abe would have gone back inside and reassured Jane that he wasn't angry with her, but he was too irritated to go back today.

"The tourists grow more annoying each year," Abe huffed to himself.

He'd been having a drink after work that evening when a pair of tourists had come rushing into the barroom, babbling about how the Bear Lake Monster had chased them in their boat.

"Almost got us," the tall scrawny boy had gasped.

"It was huge!" his girl cried.

"What did it look like?" called one of the locals from the corner, egging them on.

"Like a giant brown snake," the boy said. "It was nearly 90 feet long!"

"It had a skinny head and great big ears sticking out from the sides," the girl added. "And its mouth was big enough to eat both of us and the boat in one swallow!"

"It was a good thing we were near land," the boy concluded. "I've never rowed so fast in my life. I swear that monster was swimming a mile a minute! It went back under the water just as we reached the lily pads, and the wave it made nearly swamped the boat."

"Good thing it didn't chase you right up onto the shore," the bartender called out jovially. "They say the Bear Lake Monster has dozens of small legs, and it can scurry about on land."

"I hear it likes to sneak up on unwary swimmers and blow water at them," chortled another old-timer. "The ones it doesn't carry off to eat, that is."

All the monster talk was too much for Abe. He tossed down some money to cover his bill and stalked out to get his gun. Abe never actually shot anything when he went hunting. He mostly just walked around the lake, working out his ire until he was too tired to be mad anymore.

Abe had lived on Bear Lake all his life and had never, not once, seen any monster. His mother had been a firm believer in the monster, even though she had never seen it, while his father had been a confirmed skeptic. Abe had taken on the views of his father wholeheartedly. When Abe married a girl from out of state, he had expected her to laugh at the story of the monster. But no, Janie was as firm a believer as his mother had been.

The sky had been overcast all day. By the time Abe reached the lakeshore, the rain was drizzling down his neck. Wisps of fog were closing in on him, but Abe marched along, ignoring the weather. He wiped the moisture from his face, irritated at the rain, the tourists, the firm believers (among them his wife), and the world in general. He was especially irritated at the Bear Lake Monster itself. Stupid myth.

The fog was thicker now. If he were smart, he would go home before it became too dangerous to walk about. Reluctantly, Abe turned around, noticing as he did that a large log was floating a little way out in the lake. He would have to report it, Abe decided. The submerged log would be dangerous to boaters.

Then the log started to move. It reared up and up, rising out of the lake bed toward the cloudy sky. Abe froze in shock and disbelief. It was the Bear Lake Monster. It seemed like the monster's skinny head would touch the clouds, so far did it stretch upwards. The monster shook its head and made a funny, huffing kind of sound. Then it bent down, turning to look at the shore. Abe stumbled backward and nearly fell. The monster peered at him from its great height. Its eyes were round and dark. The monster made a kind of sniffing sound and leaned toward Abe, opening its large mouth.

The tourist girl was right. The mouth was large enough to swallow a boat, Abe thought, still in shock. As the head drew nearer, Abe realized he had to do something or he would be swallowed whole. He fumbled for his rifle, took aim, and shot at the monster one, two, three times. The monster blinked a bit, but the bullets didn't seem to bother it. Abe knew he must have hit it. He had won more trophies for his marksmanship

THE BEAR LAKE MONSTER

than Janie could keep on the fireplace mantel. But the monster didn't even notice it had been shot. It opened its mouth wide, and Abe jumped back, dropping his rifle. The monster grabbed the rifle in its mouth and swallowed it in one gulp.

Abe didn't wait around. While the Bear Lake Monster digested his rifle, he bolted away from the lake as fast as his legs would carry him. The fog was really thick now, and Abe almost ran right past his house. He slammed the door behind him and fell panting onto the sofa. Janie hurried in from the kitchen.

"Abe honey, what's wrong?" she cried.

Abe was coughing and gasping so much he couldn't speak. Janie pounded him on the back, then got him a drink of water. Abe waved it away. "Brandy," he gasped.

After several swallows, Abe finally calmed down.

"Now, tell me what happened," said Janie. "Where's your rifle?"

"I'll tell you what happened," said Abe, suddenly furious. "That Bear Lake Monster just *ate my best rifle!*"

Abe stomped upstairs and slammed the bedroom door behind him. He leaned out the window facing the shore, shook his fist at the lake and its monster, and shouted: "The next time you're hungry, you'd better eat a tourist and leave my rifle alone."

Abe sat down on the edge of the bed and took off his boots. Right then and there, he decided that he was going to start hunting somewhere else. He couldn't afford to lose another rifle to that dad-blame monster. And the next time a tourist came into the bar with a story about the Bear Lake Monster, not only would Abe believe it, he would buy the tourist a drink.

18

Divvying Up Souls

SMITH COUNTY, TEXAS

Now, Isaac wasn't afraid to walk home in the dark. No sir! He was fearless, even though the road took him right by the cemetery. So Isaac stayed late at the neighboring plantation, chatting with his friends and sweet-hearting pretty Sarah instead of hurrying home with the message he was carrying for the master.

Sarah finally shooed him off, saying he had best hurry, because the road led past the cemetery, and it was quite likely the devil would try to get him if he walked past the graveyard at night. Isaac grinned at his pretty girl and tried to steal a kiss. But she was firm with him and sent him on his way.

Isaac whistled cheerfully as he started down the road. He laughed at the strange shadows made by the trees and cackled at a chicken hurrying home to roost.

"I ain't afraid of the graveyard, not me," he chanted happily to himself, dancing a jig in the middle of the empty road.

It was full dark by the time he reached the edge of the cemetery. The stars were twinkling in the night sky. Isaac took a deep breath of the clean night air, enjoying the feel of the breeze against his face.

"Ain't no devil gonna get me," he said.

Just then, he heard the sound of voices carried to him on the breeze. Isaac was surprised to hear voices inside the graveyard at night. He peered through the darkness, but there was no one in the cemetery. The voices were coming out of thin air! Isaac's pulse quickened as he realized what he was hearing discussed in the graveyard. He paused just outside the fence to listen.

"I'll take this one, and you take that one," the voice chanted. "I'll take this one, and you take that one."

"I don't want that one. It's rotten all through," said a second voice. "That one should be yours. You like them that way."

"All right. I'll take that one. And you take this one. This one is a good one."

"I like the good ones."

"I'll take this one, and you take that one," the voice started chanting again. "I'll take this one, and you take that one."

Isaac was astonished. Sarah was right: The devil was in the graveyard tonight. And he was divvying up souls with God!

"Lord have mercy. Lord have mercy," Isaac cried. "The master will never believe this!"

Isaac hightailed it down the road as fast as he could run. He hurried right into the house and found the master.

"Master, master," he gasped. "Come quick! The devil and the good Lord are down in the cemetery divvying up souls!"

"Don't be ridiculous," his master said.

"It's true," Isaac protested. "If you don't believe me, come down to the cemetery and see for yourself!"

Divvying Up Souls

"All right," said the master. "And if I find out you were lying, I'll whip you good tomorrow morning."

The master and Isaac started out for the cemetery. As they reached the fence, the wind brought them the sound of the unearthly voices, talking to each other in the graveyard. The master was astonished when he heard the voice chanting "I'll take this one, and you take that one. I'll take this one, and you take that one."

"I don't want this one," said the second voice. "Give me that light one."

"You can have the light one. I don't want none of them anyway." The first voice resumed chanting: "I'll take this one, and you take that one."

The master and Isaac looked at one another. There was something eerie about the sound of the voices coming out of nowhere in the dark. The singsong pattern of the voices divvying up souls was mesmerizing. Isaac was not sure how long he and the master stood there listening to the devil and the good Lord talking.

Then suddenly, one of the voices said: "We nearly forgot them two over by the fence. I'll take them two, and you can have these other ones."

Isaac was petrified with fear. The devil was coming for him! He turned to look at his master, hoping the master would save him. But his master was already running up the road as fast as he could go, heading for home. Isaac followed lickety-split.

"I found them," said Ezekiel coming out from behind the fence. He was carrying the last two sweet potatoes in his hand.

Isaiah, fellow slave and thief, came up beside him. He was holding the two sacks full of sweet potatoes that they had stolen.

"Is that ol' Isaac running up the road?" Isaiah asked, staring toward the plantation.

"It sure is. Too bad he ran away so fast. I would've asked him if he wanted some sweet potatoes," said Ezekiel.

19

The Ultimate Stakes

VIRGINIA CITY, NEVADA

All was peaceful and quiet, except for the scratching of Saint Peter's quill on the scroll he was inscribing with a message for one of the archangels. I had just been assigned to fetch and carry for Saint Peter, not a bad job for minor cherubim such as myself. I had never been to the Pearly Gates before, and I found myself enjoying the view. I confess that it sometimes made me dizzy, gazing down through the clouds and dimensions, all the way to Earth.

It was nice to have a bit of peace. The last war had almost run me off my feet, and it was followed by a great earthquake somewhere in the Americas that sent a large influx of new souls to the Pearly Gates all at once. I strummed my harp, compos-ing a new melody for the great feast later that month, and try-ing to find words for my tune.

"Holy, holy, holy," I hummed to myself.

I shook my head. Those particular words featured in almost every song composed in heaven. I thought that the Lord might appreciate a different message. I tried "Justice, justice, justice," but it didn't have the same grandeur as

"Holy, holy, holy," and I decided that "Grovel, ye foolish mortal sinners" might spoil the festive mood.

"Jehosephat! Look at them gates!"

I frowned. No, those words weren't right either. Then I realized that they had been shouted from somewhere outside the realm of Heaven. I sighed and put away my harp. More souls had arrived.

"Charlie! Get a load of this!" The voice bellowed.

From somewhere below it, another voice was raised in what I think was supposed to be a song:

> *Hangtown gals are dum de . . . uh . . . rosy,*
> *Something, something, something cozy!*
> *Painted cheeks and dum dum bonnets—*
> *Something, something, sting like hornets!*

"Get up here, you crazy Argonaut!" The first voice shouted down to the second.

I followed Saint Peter past the massive, towering pearl pillars that supported the lovely gates. We stood just in front, watching as two figures weaved their way among the clouds toward us.

"What is an Argonaut?" I whispered to Saint Peter.

"Someone who sought gold in California in '49," Saint Peter replied.

I gazed at the approaching figures in horror. Miners. Great heavens. Miners!

Saint Peter gave me a reproving look.

"They may be more worthy than they appear," he said.

They appeared drunk to me. They were now dancing together. The scraggly, bearded chap wearing the lady's crinoline about his ragged pants took the woman's part, while the one with the sideburns and mustache gallantly led. They were both singing the song about Hangtown—I shuddered at the very name of such a place—but the first man didn't know the words any better than the second.

They collapsed in a heap in front of Saint Peter, laughing and waving their arms about. I shook my head. These men must have been misdirected to the Pearly Gates. Surely they had no business in Heaven.

Saint Peter frowned. "Morris . . . er . . . 'Buckshot' Smith?" he asked the man with the mustache and sideburns.

"Who wants to know?" the man asked belligerently. He rolled off the back of his companion and gazed grumpily at Saint Peter, who helped him up. Buckshot blinked and looked around him a bit. Then he brightened. "Jehosephat!" he shouted. "Just look at them gates! They must be worth a fortune! Charlie! Look at them gates."

Charlie just grunted. It appeared that he had fallen asleep in front of the Pearly Gates. Buckshot kicked him in the side, but Charlie just scratched himself and slept on.

"Charles Anthony . . . er . . . 'Grizzly Bear' Jefferson?" asked Saint Peter.

Charlie woke with a start and sat up. "Whazzat?" he mumbled as Saint Peter helped him to his feet. Charlie shook his head a few times to clear it, then gaped at Saint Peter.

"Buckshot!" Charlie shouted. "Lookie at this ripsniptious fellow. I should have worn my Sunday-go-to-meeting clothes."

"We're at the Pearly Gates, Grizzly Bear," Buckshot yelled

deafeningly. "Guess that little conbobberation we started at the bar was a bit more lively than we realized."

"They was cheating at cards!" Charlie said indignantly. Then the import of Buckshot's words penetrated his alcohol-hazed mind, and he realized where he was. Charlie straightened his crinoline and looked nervously at Saint Peter.

"Good day, sir," he said, fumbling with his hat.

"Good day, er . . . 'Grizzly Bear,' " Saint Peter replied. Buckshot was fingering the Pearly Gates. When he heard Saint Peter's greeting, he reluctantly left off and joined Charlie in front of the stand that held the Book of Names.

Saint Peter consulted the book.

"Charles Anthony Jefferson. Let me see. Lately of Virginia City. The Comstock Lode?" Saint Peter asked.

Charlie's face lit up. "Silver!" he shouted. "Silver everywhere!"

"Hasn't been a strike like it since '49!" agreed Buckshot.

"Well, Charlie, according to the book, you have been using your money to support your aged mother and have even spent some time praying in the last year or so."

"Mostly over cards!" Buckshot chortled.

"Welcome to Heaven," Saint Peter said, ignoring Buckshot's last remark.

"What about me?" asked Buckshot.

"Morris Smith. Morris Smith." Saint Peter consulted the book. "Ah, yes. Here you are. Apparently, you are almost excessively honest, which, unfortunately, is also the reason for your untimely demise, according to the book."

"Got hit in the head with a bar stool. I hate it when people cheat at three-card monte," Buckshot explained.

"Honesty is a virtue, so you are hereby welcomed into Heaven," said Saint Peter.

I watched dubiously as the two Comstock miners whooped and hollered and danced their way through the Pearly Gates.

"Are you sure about this?" I asked Saint Peter.

"Their names are in the Great Book," he replied. He headed back into the gatehouse to finish his letter.

I stood there for a few moments more, pondering the imponderable mysteries of Heaven. The entrance of those two miners into the Holy Realm surely was one of the biggest mysteries I had ever encountered.

Through the gates, I heard a shout.

"Gold! Gold!" bellowed Buckshot.

"Eureka!" Grizzly Bear shouted.

Apparently, the miners had just noticed that they were waltzing up the streets of gold.

I sighed and went into the gatehouse to finish my song. After this latest encounter, I reconsidered using "Grovel, ye foolish mortal sinners" as the opening line. I wondered if the words were strong enough to stifle the Comstock miners. Outside, I heard the sounds of enthusiastic digging. Buckshot called, "Help me haul up this brick, Grizzly Bear." No, definitely not strong enough.

Over the next several days, the Comstock miners did their best to make a complete mess of Heaven. The street from the Pearly Gates to the front of their mansion was staked out and full of holes where they had managed to pry up the gold bricks. The silver fountain had been dismantled and now stood in pieces in the front of the miners' house. The jeweled walls

THE ULTIMATE STAKES

surrounding the temple were missing many priceless diamonds, rubies, and emeralds. And somehow, the miners had located the wine cellars and had drunk enough wine to kill them, if they weren't already dead.

So it was with great trepidation that I noticed that the next soul to approach the Pearly Gates was another miner. Saint Peter looked as worried as I felt. The grizzled old man stopped in front of the stand and took off his hat.

"Daniel Gillespie?" asked Saint Peter.

"Yes, indeed," said the miner.

"You are from Virginia City. You were a miner at the Comstock Lode."

"That's right," said Daniel.

"It says here you died in the mines."

"Got careless around some orphan elixir," said Daniel calmly.

I glanced curiously at Saint Peter.

"He fell afoul of some nitroglycerin," Saint Peter interpreted for me.

"Blew myself to kingdom come," Daniel said cheerfully.

"Well, Daniel," Saint Peter continued, "according to the Book of Names, you have worshipped God under the stars at night, played fair with everyone, and always worked hard for your grub stakes. So, I guess I have to let you into Heaven." Saint Peter sighed.

"I thank you kindly, sir," said Daniel. "But tell me, why are you so reluctant to let me into Heaven?"

"Well, Daniel, two of your fellow Comstock miners arrived here last week, and they have been tearing up the golden streets," said Saint Peter.

Daniel smiled. "I can take care of that easily enough," he said. He thanked Saint Peter again and walked jauntily through the Pearly Gates into Heaven.

I wondered what he could possibly do to make Buckshot and Grizzly Bear behave. I decided that he was just boasting.

To my great surprise, the next morning brought Buckshot and Grizzly Bear back to the Pearly Gates. They were carrying sacks full of gold bricks. They applied to Saint Peter to be released from Heaven. Saint Peter was astonished. He warned them that once they left, they could not return. This didn't seem to bother Buckshot and Grizzly Bear. So Saint Peter released them, and they wound their way down the clouds, carrying their gold bricks and singing a song with words that were much too naughty for me to repeat.

Saint Peter and I were terribly curious about the matter. Saint Peter sent me to find out from the third Comstock miner exactly what had caused Buckshot and Grizzly Bear to leave Heaven. I found Daniel taking his ease in a plaza paved with amethyst stones. I sat next to him and asked him how he arranged for the removal of the other miners. Daniel chuckled and slapped his knee with his battered old hat.

"It was easy," he said. "I just told them that there was a rich new strike in Hell. They couldn't get out of here fast enough!"

A new strike! I was amazed. I should have thought of that myself. I thanked Daniel and hurried back to relate the news to Saint Peter.

Life in Heaven became serene once again. I finished my song, and Saint Peter left me in charge of the Pearly Gates while he went to visit with Saint John and Saint Paul. I had just admitted a pious nun whose list of good works took up three pages in the Book of Names when Daniel came through the Pearly Gates.

"Daniel," I said. "What brings you here?"

"Well," Daniel said. "I would like to leave Heaven."

"Leave Heaven?" I exclaimed. "Why?"

"I got to thinking about that new strike in Hell," Daniel explained. "I'd like to get down there and stake out a few good claims before the rush."

I was amazed. Seeing that he was in earnest, I cautioned him that he could never return and let him go. What else could I do?

As soon as Saint Peter returned, I told him of Daniel's defection. Saint Peter took the news philosophically. He sighed, shook his head, then went back to work. I was not so sanguine.

"I don't understand," I lamented to Saint Peter. "Why would anyone leave Heaven for Hell?"

Saint Peter said: "I am afraid that it happens more often than you think. Once a miner, always a miner."

20

Juan's Last Drink

Oh my, but Juan was a drinking man. If there was any drink to be had in house or town, Juan was sure to find it and would be as drunk as a lord before you knew it. How his good wife, Maria, put up with him, I don't know. She brought Juan to church in Albuquerque every week, and the Padre would admonish him over and over to mend his ways. The devil, said the Padre, would come for Juan's soul if he did not stop his drinking. Maria wailed and clasped her rosary beads in despair when she heard this pronouncement, but Juan just laughed.

"The devil, he will not get me," Juan boasted.

So Juan continued his drinking. He drank wine at home, and he drank beer with his neighbors. One afternoon he visited his friend who was the *alcalde* (mayor) of a town outside Albuquerque, and they sat in the local bar drinking hard liquor and talking all afternoon.

The *alcalde* and Juan staggered out of the bar just before dusk. The *alcalde* handed Juan a half-empty bottle of whiskey and made his way home, walking a little too straight and a little too careful. Juan wove up to his wagon, carefully placed the bottle of whiskey on the seat, then tried to climb up the side of his horse. He promptly slid off the other side of the horse and lay blinking up at the darkening sky. Finally, Juan remembered that his horse was attached to a wagon, so he climbed up the side of the wagon and stumbled his way into the seat.

Juan pointed his horse west, hoping the animal would know how to get home. Then he finished drinking up the bottle of whiskey, singing boisterously as he drove. When the bottle was empty, Juan tossed it over the side of the wagon. Immediately, the bottle reversed direction and hit him on the head. Wham! Juan clutched his head and stared at the empty bottle at his feet. Carefully, Juan picked it up and threw it over the side of the wagon. Wham! It hit him in the head again.

As Juan reached for the bottle a third time, he saw something out of the corner of his eye. An elegantly dressed man was sitting on a gilded chair in the back of the wagon. Juan was stunned. He knew there had been no man and no chair when he climbed up to his seat. He turned quickly to look behind him. The back of the wagon was empty! Juan faced front and leaned down toward the bottle at his feet, glancing behind him out of the corner of his eye. There was the man again.

The man was obviously a caballero, for he was dressed in the finest black silk with elaborate silver trim. He was pulling on a pair of gloves. Juan's heart started pounding fast when he saw that the man had long claws rather than fingers.

Just then Juan heard a friendly shout from the side of the road. He sat erect and looked over at Rico, who was cleaning up his tools after mending a fence on his property.

"Juan! What brings you home so late? Does Maria know you were drinking with the *alcalde?*"

"Maria thinks I went to town on business," Juan called back with a forced laugh. "Say, amigo, do you see a man in the back of my wagon?"

Rico laughed heartily. "Your wagon is as empty as your head, Juan! If you are seeing things back there, it is time to go home! Anyway, Maria will be worried. It is almost dark."

Rico waved and smiled as Juan drove past him. As soon as he was out of sight, Juan reached again for the bottle, peering through the corner of his eye into the back of the wagon. The man in black silk was still sitting on the elegant chair, but now he stared mockingly at Juan with eyes of red fire. Juan gulped and sat up very straight. He did not know what to do. The devil was riding in the wagon with him!

Juan turned his head a bit, looking back over his left shoulder. The devil gave him a slight smile and beckoned to him with one black-gloved hand. Juan gave an involuntarily jerk on the reins. His horse whinnied in protest and stopped. Juan glanced back again. The devil stood up and stepped toward him.

Juan let out a terrified yell that spooked his horse. Juan pulled the plunging horse to a stop, leaped out of the wagon, and fell to his knees.

"Hail Mary, full of grace. The Lord is with you," Juan prayed desperately. "Blessed are you among women."

JUAN'S LAST DRINK

He could clearly see the devil now, standing in the back of the wagon, beckoning for Juan to come up and join him. Juan closed his eyes and said the Hail Mary over and over again. It was the only prayer he could remember in his panic.

After several minutes of loud praying, Juan heard the wagon creak as the devil stepped down to the ground. Juan gasped, scuttling away on his knees, still saying Hail Marys. The devil frowned at Juan. Juan said another Hail Mary. The devil shook his head angrily and walked away.

Juan kept saying Hail Marys until the devil was out of sight. Then he jumped into the wagon and raced toward home. Just before Juan reached his farm, the empty bottle of whiskey rose up from the floor of the wagon and bashed him in the head.

Juan let out a terrified whimper and looked behind him, expecting to see the devil. Standing in the back of the wagon was a beautiful angel dressed all in white. The angel was staring at him disapprovingly. The angel pointed to the empty whiskey bottle. It rose up into the air and hit Juan in the head again.

"If you don't stop drinking," the angel said, making the bottle bounce off Juan's head with each word, "there is no prayer on this earth that can save you from the devil."

The angel disappeared, and the bottle clattered to the floor of the wagon.

Juan never took a drink again.

21

The Bucca

VIRGINIA CITY, NEVADA

The missus and I had only been in the New World for two years when they struck silver out in Nevada.

"Mark my words, Jack," said the missus, "those green-horns are going to need help mining that silver. You've spent your whole life working the mines back home in Cornwall. You're going to have to go out there and show them how to do it right."

I was reluctant at first. I was comfortably retired after a lifetime spent in the mines, and I wasn't looking to go back. But it soon became obvious that the Yanks knew nothing about hard-rock mining. They were always letting unwanted persons come onto their diggings, something a Cornish man would never do. That will jinx you for sure.

Then one day, I heard a fellow talking about miners killing rats in the mines. Killing rats! I was horrified. Those stupid greenhorns didn't even know that rats can sense a cave-in before it happens. "When the rats move out, so does the miner" is an inflexible rule in mining. If you watch the rats, you know which way to run.

That story decided me. The missus and I packed up and went to Nevada. The missus always comes with me. She was a miner's daughter before she became a miner's wife, and if any woman could tame a wild bunch like the Yankee miners, it was my missus.

We settled in Virginia City, and the greenhorns were in awe of us right from the get-go. The ease with which I discovered new veins of silver made them think that I could smell the ore. Thirty years of experience in the mines might have helped, but I wasn't about to spoil the legend growing up around me and the other Cornish miners who began condescending to teach the greenhorns about mining.

The first thing I taught the greenhorns around me was to watch the candles. If the candles go out, you go out too. A candle won't burn in bad air. If your candle flickers out, you are probably on the point of asphyxiation. Also, no whistling in the mines. Sharp sounds cause vibrations, and vibrations cause cave-ins.

Of course, the most important thing to know about mining is that you should always stay on the good side of the Bucca (what the English call "Tommy Knockers"), the spirits of departed miners. The Bucca, when they are visible, take the form of little old men. They have small bodies and big ugly heads with big ears and noses. They wear peaked hats, leather jackets, and water-soaked leather boots.

The Bucca help miners find ore. They also knock on the walls of the mines right before a cave-in. They have saved the life of many a miner. Of course, the very first man to hear the sound was jinxed. He would be the first to die either in the disaster or just following it, unless he quit the mines altogether.

We Cornish miners were right thankful of the Bucca, and always left pastries and cakes and other food for them. Any greenhorn who made them angry would be sure to lose his hat, his tools, or his pipe and tobacco. Sometimes he would be hit in the head with a rock, aimed by a surly Bucca. If a Bucca got really mad with a chap, it would blow out his candles or tamper with his dynamite fuses. If this happened too often, it was always best to leave the Bucca a nice meal and maybe make a small clay image of the Bucca to appease it.

Shortly after we arrived in Nevada, the missus and I made friends with a couple of Welshmen named Ned and Terry. They were quite a pair of tricksters, yes sir! It got so bad that no one would believe anything they said, because if they did, Ned and Terry would make them look foolish. But Ned and Terry were popular. We miners dearly loved a laugh after a hard day working in the mine.

One evening, Ned and Terry decided to work the late shift. As they descended into the mine, they began hearing the sound of hammers striking a drill, punctuated by the sound of voices. Neither man recognized the voices, so they assumed it was some new chaps working the late shift. Ned and Terry grinned at each other. They liked pulling jokes on newcomers.

Ned and Terry followed the sound of the hammers and came into a shaft flickering with the light of a single lantern. They were amazed to see two hammers floating in midair, striking the head of a rusty old drill that was rotating itself. They could hear a murmur of voices but could see no one.

THE BUCCA

Giving a startled yell, Ned and Terry beat a hasty retreat. Climbing to the top of the mine, they gasped out the story to me and a few of my mates who were lifting glasses at the local saloon. None of us would believe them. It was just the sort of practical joke we'd learned to avoid.

Finally, Ned and Terry grabbed me and another fellow and dragged us, protesting, down into the mine. When we entered the shaft, the invisible hands were still hard at work, hammering at the drill as they talked to each other. I recognized them at once, and my blood turned ice cold.

"Bucca," I gasped. Stupid fools. There was no way I wanted to disturb the Bucca. Bad luck was sure to follow. Maybe even death. I grabbed Ned's arm. "Let's get out of here!"

We backed out of the shaft as quietly as possible so as not to disturb the spirit workers. Then we hurried up into the starlight.

I went back to the shaft the next morning with a small image of a Bucca and some food. No bad luck was going to follow me around just because two fools stumbled on the Bucca at work.

Ned and Terry were spooked for several weeks following the incident. They were convinced that they would be the next ones to die, since they had disturbed the Bucca. But day after day passed and nothing happened, so eventually they regained their high spirits and were just as quick to play jokes on us as before. We thought all was well. Then, two months to the day, we got word of a major cave-in. Ned and Terry were both killed.

It never pays to disturb the Bucca.

22

The Singing Sands

SAND MOUNTAIN RECREATION AREA, NEVADA

Many years ago, when the world was newer than it is today, though still quite old, much of Nevada was underneath a great inland sea. Within that sea dwelt many creatures, swimming and playing and fighting and doing what all creatures do to survive and thrive in this world. Giant dolphin-like mammals called ichthyosaurs swam through these waters, and plesiosaurs with their long necks and large bodies also called this sea their home.

Then the sea began to dry up, and the waters receded from the land. In ones and twos and sometimes in large groups, the creatures of the great sea found themselves stranded in shallow water that disappeared around them. But two plesiosaurs that were a little quicker, a little smarter, and a little more maneuverable than their fellows made their way through the drying sea into the deepest section of the water.

When the sea was gone, the two plesiosaurs were the only ones left alive out of all their kind. They lived deep beneath the waters of Walker Lake, swimming, eating, and playing together. They were content because they had each other, and for a time they needed nothing else.

Then one day, a harsh, strong wind began to blow and blow across the newly revealed land. The wind thoroughly dried out the old seabed, sweeping dirt and sand before it and rearranging the landscape as it pleased. Deep beneath the surface of Walker Lake, the plesiosaurs were frightened by the keening of the great wind and the violent stirring of the surface water. They swam into the depths to wait out the storm.

The terrible windstorm raged for many days, longer than the worst storm of its kind. Down at the bottom of the lake, the plesiosaurs grew used to the sound of the wind buffeting the top of the lake and keening across the land. The female plesiosaur soon forgot the danger such a windstorm held for her, and only remembered the joy she took in riding the waves when Walker Lake had been a part of that much larger sea. So great was her longing to frolic and play again among the waves, that she swam to the surface and emerged from the protection of the water into the stormy wind.

The large waves buffeted her, and for a moment she gloried in their strength. She did not see the whirlwind until it was upon her. It sucked her up out of the water, swirling her around and around. Her body was buffeted by the tons of sand picked up by the harsh wind, and she was swept northward, away from the lake and her mate. When the whirlwind subsided suddenly, it buried the female plesiosaur beneath tons and tons of sand that formed a giant dune.

Alone and dying underneath the Sand Mountain that was created by the whirlwind, the female plesiosaur called and called out in agony for her mate. Around her, the sands echoed

THE SINGING SANDS

and sang a beautiful song, comforting her pain. Somewhere deep in Walker Lake, another lonely plesiosaur keened in response.

Through the ages from then until now, animals and humans have lived in the land that was once beneath a great sea, eating, drinking, loving, raising their children, and dying in the great cycle of life. And still the Sand Mountain stands among the Sand Springs Mountains, a graceful reminder of the great sea that once occupied the land and of the terrible windstorm that created the dunes. They say that when the wind blows strongly against the Sand Mountain, the spirit of the female plesiosaur is reminded of the waves she once rode on the great sea in joyful play with her mate, and she keens and moans, calling to him again and again. Around her, the sands echo and sing, comforting her pain. And somewhere deep beneath Walker Lake, the spirit of the male plesiosaur keens in response.

23

Old Granny Tucker

TYLER, TEXAS

There were just the three of us when I was growing up—
Mama, Nicholas, and me. My name is Carrie. Papa died when
Nicholas was two and I was five. I barely remembered him.
There were no other relatives on Papa's side of the family, and
the only relative we had on Mama's side was old Granny
Tucker, whom we never saw. So we were all alone in the world,
and Mama had to work hard as a seamstress to keep food on
the table and a roof over our heads.

When I was a little girl, I never thought about Granny
Tucker. I was too busy playing with Nicholas and helping Mama
around the house. But as I grew older, I began wondering why
we never saw her. She lived just outside the village, only a few
miles from our little house. Other families visited back and
forth with their relatives, even when they lived far apart. But
Mama never talked about Granny Tucker, and she never took
us to visit her.

I wanted to ask Mama about her, but somehow I could
never get the words out. Whenever Mama heard one of our
neighbors mention Granny Tucker, her lips thinned, and she

frowned fiercely. I was very curious, and so I started eaves-
dropping on conversations anytime I heard the name Tucker
mentioned.

It did not take me long to realize why Mama frowned
whenever she heard her mother's name. Granny Tucker was a
witch. From what I overheard, the townsfolk often visited
Granny Tucker's cottage to buy love potions or to ask her to
hex someone who offended them. They also blamed her for
everything that went wrong, from spoiled stews to missing
animals. They said that Granny Tucker could find anyone she
wanted to hex, even if they hid from her. She had a magic ball
that she used to find people, and it was never wrong.

One day, I listened to a few neighborhood women talking
in the dry goods store about Granny. One woman described
the way Granny would shed her skin at night and her spirit
would fly on the evening wind. When she returned to her
home before dawn, she would say, "Skin, skin, let me in."
Then she would slide back into her skin and be a woman again.
Another spoke of Granny turning herself into a cat and
roaming over the land doing evil things. The third woman
spoke of the children living with Granny Tucker. No one knew
where they came from or who they were or if they really
belonged to Granny, since she was not married. I saw the
woman glance toward me as she spoke, and I knew she was
thinking about Mama.

As I walked home with my packages, I wondered how
Mama had managed to escape Granny Tucker without being
cursed. Then I thought of how Papa had died so young, and I
wondered if she really had escaped. I talked the matter over

with Nicholas, who is very wise. He thought that Papa must have bribed Granny Tucker somehow, and that is why she allowed him to marry Mama. Neither of us had enough nerve to ask Mama about it.

Nicholas and I were very curious to see Granny Tucker. I wanted to judge for myself whether or not she was a witch. She might, I told Nicholas, just be some poor misunderstood old woman. Nicholas laughed when I said that. He was sure she was a witch, and he wanted to see her do magic.

Finally, I worked up enough courage to ask Mama if Nicholas and I could visit our grandmother. As soon as she heard my question, Mama turned pale and clutched at the doorframe. For a long moment, she didn't speak. I stood waiting nervously for her response.

"You want to visit your grandmother?" she asked, sitting down abruptly on a kitchen chair.

"Yes, Mama," I replied. "Nicholas and I can walk to her house after school and spend the night."

"Carrie, I cannot allow you to go," Mama said. "No child has ever returned from that house except me. And your father had to pay Mother a hundred dollars for me before she let me go."

So Nicholas was right, I thought.

I didn't say anything more that day. But every day after that, either Nicholas or I would ask Mama if we could visit Granny Tucker. Mama was afraid for us, I knew. But I would not be satisfied with rumors. I had to see for myself what kind of grandmother I had. Nicholas felt the same way.

Finally, Mama said we could visit Granny Tucker on the following Saturday. Mama spent every night that week teaching us all the spells that she had learned when she lived with Granny, so we could protect ourselves should the need arise. It was the first time Mama had ever admitted that she knew magic.

Nicholas also devised an escape plan, just in case anything went wrong. He said to Mama, "I am going to put the dogs into a pen next to the house. If anything happens to Carrie or me, I will whistle the magic spell you taught us. When the dogs hear it, they will bark. Let them out when they bark, and they will come and rescue us."

A little of the tension left Mama's face when she heard Nicholas's plan. I hated making Mama worry, but I was determined to visit Granny Tucker.

We left our house around noon, and after walking for an hour, we came up to Granny's gate. I saw Granny Tucker at once. She was a little bent old woman with white hair and wicked black eyes. She was digging in a twisted little garden at the side of her house. She straightened up and looked right at us. She knew who we were and welcomed us by name.

"So, Carrie and Nicholas have come at last to visit with their old granny," she said.

There was nothing terrible about her words, but something in her tone gave me goose bumps. I glanced at Nicholas. He was regarding Granny Tucker calmly. Nothing ever upset Nicholas.

"Good day, Granny Tucker," I said, curtsying politely.

Granny beckoned for us to come into her garden. We walked through the gate and met Granny on the walk in front of her house. She studied us with a little smile that made me

OLD GRANNY TUCKER

want to run away. Then she called her children to come and meet us and sent us into the back pasture to play.

I didn't like Granny's children. There was a boy my age and a girl who was a little younger than Nicholas. They both had a sly look in their eyes, and their skin had a little too much hair. They had strange ears that ended in a point, and when they smiled, their teeth were pointed and looked very sharp.

The children didn't know any of the games we played at school. They were very rough and didn't seem to mind hurting us. I think they liked hearing us cry out in pain when they knocked us down or stepped on our feet. Nicholas hated them from the moment he saw them. Nicholas is always very formal and polite with people he hates. By the time we went in to supper, Nicholas was speaking in such a formal manner that he sounded like a politician.

After supper, Granny Tucker sat in a corner, sharpening her knife. She asked Nicholas to turn the grindstone for her. When Nicholas asked her what she was going to do with the knife, Granny replied, "I am going to kill a wild hog I have penned outside."

I had seen nothing in the pen except a few chicken feathers. My heart gave a frightened little leap. Nicholas's face became inscrutable. Whenever Nicholas looked like that, it meant he was worried.

Once the knife was sharpened, Granny Tucker had me fill the large pot with water and hang it over the fire to boil. Then she sent us all to bed in the loft. She put her two children in one pallet, covered with a dark sheet. Then she put Nicholas and me into the other pallet and covered us with a white sheet.

Granny's children fell asleep right away. They grunted and snorted in their sleep like a pair of animals. I knew I would not sleep that night, but I pretended to doze. Nicholas just lay with his eyes wide open, staring at the ceiling. Finally, Granny asked him why he didn't go to sleep. Nicholas said, "Mama always lets me play the fiddle before bed. Playing the fiddle helps me relax."

Granny Tucker took the fiddle down from its place over the mantelpiece and gave it to Nicholas. He started playing softly, sweet lullabies and gentle songs about love. As he played, I watched Granny Tucker. She sat near the steps, waiting patiently for Nicholas to fall asleep. I saw her fingering something hidden under her apron. I knew it was the sharpened knife. I was so frightened I could hardly breathe. Beside me, Nicholas played the fiddle better than he had ever played it before. I knew he was frightened too. Downstairs, Granny Tucker's head began to nod. At last, she fell asleep in her chair.

Nicholas put down the fiddle and motioned for me to get out of bed. While Nicholas removed the dark sheet from the sleeping children, I placed several bundles in our pallet to make it look like two people were sleeping there. We covered our pallet with the dark sheet and put the white sheet over Granny's children. Then we snuck down the stairs and out the door into the moonlight.

As soon as we were out of sight of the house, we ran as fast as we could go. It was not long before we heard a shriek of rage and horror coming from the house. Granny Tucker must have used the sharp knife on the children under the white sheet, not knowing until now that they were her own.

Nicholas grabbed my hand, and we ran even faster, taking side roads and twisting back and forth so as not to be found. I was winded and had a cramp in my side, but I did not dare stop. I kept remembering Granny's magic ball that could track anyone. If we did not reach our house soon, then Granny would track us down and kill us.

Suddenly, I heard a rumbling behind us. I looked back and saw a glowing ball following us in the moonlight.

"She's found us," I called to Nicholas. He nodded, too breathless to speak. Then he pulled me over to a large tree and thrust me up into the branches. I climbed up as fast as I could go, right to the top. Nicholas gave the emergency whistle for his dogs and then climbed up after me.

I could hear Granny Tucker muttering angrily to herself as she came down the road. She had a clear view of us silhouetted against the moonlit sky and came right to the bottom of our tree. She was carrying an ax. I hoped with all my heart that Mama had heard the dogs barking and turned them loose. It was our only chance.

Below us, Granny Tucker started chopping down the tree. With each blow she chanted: "Wham, bam, jenny-mo-jam. Wham, bam, jenny-mo-jam."

I closed my eyes, remembering one of the spells Mama taught us. "Tree, tree, when the ax goes 'chop,' grow big at the bottom, grow little at the top," I sang.

"It's working," Nicholas said, gazing down at Granny Tucker. "The chopped bits are growing back. Keep singing!"

So I kept singing, "Tree, tree, when the ax goes 'chop,' grow big at the bottom, grow little at the top." Below us,

Granny kept chanting, "Wham, bam, jenny-mo-jam. Wham, bam, jenny-mo-jam." She was chopping as fast as she could.

Then I heard the baying of Nicholas's hounds. They came running up the road in a bunch and attacked Granny Tucker. A terrible fight ensued. Granny slashed at the dogs with the ax, and when she dropped that, she took out the sharp knife. One, two, three dogs fell to the ground, dead from stab wounds. She cut the throat of the fourth. Nicholas was shouting and cursing Granny, tears running down his cheeks as he watched his dogs die. Goldie, the oldest hound and Nicholas's first pet, had been at the back of the pack when they attacked. She was too old to keep up with the younger dogs. But she saw her chance when Granny slashed the throats of two of the younger dogs. Goldie leaped upon her and tore out her throat. Granny Tucker flailed about for a moment longer with her knife, then died.

Nicholas was so distraught by the slaughter that I had to drag him down out of the tree. As Nicholas sat weeping between the bodies of two of his hounds, I knelt beside Granny and took her knife. Mama had taught us one spell that good people should not use. But in this case, I thought I could make an exception.

The thought of what I had to do made my stomach heave, but I gritted my teeth and cut out Granny Tucker's heart. Goldie lay nearby, nuzzling the corpse of one of her pups. She whined a little as I took Granny's heart and walked over to her. I rubbed the heart on the dead pup's nose and watched as the hound came back to life. Quickly, I did the same for all the dogs. Nicholas observed me in silence. When they were all alive again, I dropped the heart to the ground, ran into the bushes, and was sick. When I was done being sick, Nicholas led me over to a nearby stream so I could wash off that wicked woman's blood. Then he and the dogs took me home.

Mama and Nicholas went back the next day and buried Granny and the children. They told the neighbors that the whole household had died of scarlet fever. No one questioned the truth of this statement. I think the whole neighborhood was relieved that they were gone.

I was ill for a week following that night. Once I was out of danger, I had a long talk with Mama, and then with the priest. I never did magic again.

24

The Spirit on the Mountain

GILA COUNTY, ARIZONA

There was once an old grandmother living with her two grandchildren near a steep mountain. They were quite alone, for their closest neighbors lived miles away. But they were happy together and loved their home, so they stayed in the shadow of the mountain far away from the rest of the world.

The children were allowed to play in the valley near their home, but the old grandmother would never let them climb up the mountain. "An evil spirit dwells there," she told them, "and it is looking for a body to inhabit so it can come back to the land of the living." The children were frightened by her words and promised to avoid the mountain slopes and stay near the house.

To protect them further, the old grandmother taught her grandchildren a spell that would let them transform themselves into everyday objects. If the evil spirit ever came to their home while she was away, the children could hide from it and be safe. When the grandmother returned, she would drive away the evil spirit and use a counterspell to transform the children back to their human shapes.

One day, the little brother became ill with a terrible fever. His sister and grandmother did everything they could to make him well, but his fever would not break. Finally, the old grandmother told the children that she had to climb the mountain to gather some rare herbs that would make the little brother well.

The sister was frightened.

"What about the evil spirit, Grandmother?" she cried. "It will kill you and take over your body."

"I am very strong," said the old grandmother, "and I know many spells. The spirit will not catch me."

The sister begged her not to make such a dangerous climb, but the grandmother refused to listen. She set out early the next morning, chanting a protection spell as she walked and using her cane to help her over the rough spots. She climbed up and up the steep mountain, over sharp rocks and debris, determined to locate the herbs that would make her grandson well.

It was late in the afternoon when the grandmother reached a sunny ledge just below the summit of the mountain. Her body ached, and she had many scrapes on her hands and her feet from the sharp rocks. But the grandmother hardly noticed these pains, for she could see one of the rare herbs she sought growing just in front of her. She bent over, grabbed the top of the plant, and gave a tug. The plant came out of the ground so fast that she fell off the ledge and started rolling down the mountain with the herb clutched in her hand.

The evil spirit had been waiting for just such a moment. It shook the whole top of the mountain in its glee, causing dirt

THE SPIRIT ON THE MOUNTAIN

and stones to cascade down the mountain, burying the old grandmother. By the time the rockslide reached the bottom of the mountain, she was dead.

The evil spirit swooped down upon the debris and took over the old grandmother's body. It cackled delightedly to itself, pleased with its new home. It stood up, shook the dirt and stones off its body, and started walking toward the old grandmother's home. It was determined to feast on the children before dark. It carried the rare herbs in its hand and sang a cheerful song as it walked, hoping to fool the children long enough to get within striking range.

Back at the house, the sister was waiting anxiously for the grandmother to return. Around midday, the little brother's fever had broken, and there was no need for the healing herbs that had sent the old grandmother on such a dangerous journey. As the little brother lay fast asleep in his bed, the sister paced up and down the small house, listening for her grandmother's footsteps.

It was almost dark when the sister heard the sound of singing and recognized her grandmother's voice. But the voice sounded strange and hollow, like something dead. The girl knew then that her grandmother had perished on the mountain, and the evil spirit was coming to kill them. Frightened, she locked the door and took her brother into the back room.

When the evil spirit arrived, it was confused by the locked door and ran around and around the outside of the house, looking for a way in. The children were terrified. The sister knew they would have to transform themselves in order to escape from the evil spirit. But there was no grandmother to remove the spell, and the nearest neighbors were many miles away.

"We must use Grandmother's spell, little brother," said the sister, "and pray that someone will find us and return us to our bodies after the evil spirit is gone."

The sister chanted the spell and transformed herself into a small stone, which her brother hid beneath the bed. Then the little brother sat down beside the fireplace and transformed himself into a log.

When the evil spirit broke into the house and came looking for the children, they were nowhere to be seen. It called and called to them, using their grandmother's voice, but there was no answer. After searching for many hours, the evil spirit left the house, never to return.

For many long years, the evil spirit haunted the slopes of the mountain, luring the unwary into its clutches, while the house at the foot of the mountain slowly crumbled away. Inside the house, a small stone and a log waited patiently for someone to come and transform them back to their bodies. But no one ever came.

25

Death and the Doctor

SANTA CRUZ COUNTY, ARIZONA

My uncle Caleb was the most successful doctor in three counties. He was called out to every emergency, and he was the favored doctor of both the rich and the poor. If he said someone was going to live, then they lived. But if he said they were going to die, there was nothing you could do for them except call for the priest. Uncle Caleb never charged a dime for the people who were going to die. Everyone thought he was wonderful.

I was eight years old when I got scarlet fever. I had a very bad case and was delirious for many hours. Uncle Caleb was away tending some rich man up in Tucson when I fell ill, and Mama sent word for him to come quickly. Papa sat beside me, bathing my forehead with water, and Mama paced up and down, looking out the window for Uncle Caleb. I kept tossing and turning, unable to get comfortable. As time passed, I became aware of a tall, cloaked figure standing at the foot of my bed. Mama passed right by it without a glance. Papa also did not see the figure. He kept bathing my head with cool water, trying to give me some relief.

I closed my eyes, too tired to watch, too feverish to sleep. Every time I opened my eyes, the figure was still there. I

DEATH AND THE DOCTOR

couldn't summon enough strength to ask Papa about it. Suddenly, Mama gave a glad cry and ran out of the room. I could hear her talking to my Uncle Caleb as he climbed the stairs. He hurried into my room, and his very presence seemed to radiate strength and vitality. He looked straight at the cloaked figure standing at the foot of my bed and gave a little nod. Then he gently pushed Papa to one side and examined me.

"Teresa will live," he told my parents. Mama wept for joy, and Papa kept shaking Uncle Caleb's hand. I wondered how it was that Uncle Caleb could see the figure at the bottom of my bed when Mama and Papa could not. I wanted to ask him about it, but instead I fell asleep.

I did not see Uncle Caleb again until Easter. He came to stay with us for the holiday, and when we were alone, I asked him about the figure I had seen at the foot of my bed. Uncle Caleb looked grave. "You saw Lady Death at the foot of your bed, Teresa," he said. "Whenever someone is ill, Lady Death attends them. When she stands at the foot of the bed, the person can be cured. If she stands at the head of the bed, then the person will surely die."

"How do you know this?" I asked. "How is it you and I could see her, but Mama and Papa could not?"

"It is a gift that has been passed down in our family for many generations," said Uncle Caleb. "The family members who can see Lady Death generally become doctors."

I thought about this. "Must I be a doctor?" I asked.

"You may be whatever you wish," Uncle Caleb said.

"How did we get such a gift?" I asked.

"I was told by your grandmother, who also had this gift, that a particularly pious ancestor of ours was blessed with spirit sight as a reward for his fair treatment of all people, rich and poor. Spirit sight is the gift of seeing the invisible.

"One day, while our ancestor was cooking dinner over an open fire outside his house, an old man walked by and asked him for a bite. Our ancestor recognized the old man immediately—it was Saint Peter walking the earth in disguise to test the good and punish the evil. He said to Saint Peter, 'I will not give you a bite, Saint Peter, because you do not treat the poor as well as you do the rich. The rich have so much, but the poor have nothing at all.' Recognizing the justice of his words, Saint Peter walked away.

"A second man approached the fire just as our ancestor was taking the chicken off the spit. He asked for a bite. Our ancestor recognized him as Saint Anthony. He said, 'I will not give you a bite, Saint Anthony, because your bishops receive so many offerings, but they do not share the money with the poor.' Recognizing the justice of his words, Saint Anthony walked away.

"As our ancestor sat down with his meal, a woman came to the fire and asked him for a bite. Our ancestor recognized her as Lady Death. He immediately handed her a chicken leg, saying, 'Please take and eat of my chicken, Lady Death. You do not play favorites, but take the souls of both rich and poor.'

"For this kindness, Lady Death rewarded our ancestor and some of his descendants with the gift of spirit sight. For many generations, members of our family have been careful to use their gift for the good of mankind, and not for personal gain. The only exception was your great-uncle Ezra, who became tempted by wealth. His greed was the death of him.

"Ezra was called to the bedside of a very rich man. When he entered the room, he saw Lady Death standing at the head of the bed. Ezra immediately told the man's wife that he was beyond aid. The woman begged him to save her husband, and she offered him one thousand silver dollars to cure him. One thousand dollars was a lot of money in those days, and Ezra accepted her offer. He began to chant nonsense words and waved his hands over the sick man. Then he walked slowly around the bed. When he reached the head, he pushed Lady Death to the foot. Then he treated the man for his illness.

"When the man was healed, Ezra took the thousand silver dollars from the man's grateful wife and carried them to his home. He slept with them under his pillow that night. He wakened once and put his hand under the pillow to feel the coins. The movement disturbed his wife, and she looked at Ezra and sat up with a gasp. 'Who is that?' she cried, pointing toward the head of the bed. Ezra looked and saw Lady Death standing there. He turned pale and collapsed back against his pillow, dead from a heart attack. The bag of silver was still clutched in his hand. Lady Death nodded once to his wife, then disappeared.

"Since that day, no one in our family who has the gift of spirit sight has dared to use it for personal gain," Uncle Caleb said.

We sat in silence for a few moments. "I think," I said at last, "that I will become a doctor like you, Uncle Caleb."

"Just don't make the same mistake as Great-Uncle Ezra," he warned me.

"I won't," I said. And I never did.

26

The Skeleton

BERNALILLO COUNTY, NEW MEXICO

The boy had been out looking for work all day. When night fell, he was far from home. He searched for a place to sleep and found an empty, rundown house. Although it looked as if it would break apart at any moment, at least it offered some shelter, and he went inside. He was very tired, so he lay down on the floor to rest and fell into a sound sleep.

The boy was awakened quite suddenly by a thump on the roof. With a pounding heart, he sat up and lit a candle. He could see nothing above him, but then a voice called out, "I'm falling down!"

The boy scrambled out of the way just as a skeletal arm came crashing to the floor. The voice shouted again, "I'm falling down!" and another arm landed beside the first. Next came a leg, then the chest, then a second leg. Before he could count to ten, a complete skeleton was standing in front of him, grinning madly.

The boy lifted his chin and grinned back, determined not to show his fear.

The skeleton was delighted by the boy's spirit and said, "You have courage, son. Are you brave enough to wrestle me?"

The boy was terrified. He did not want to touch a skeleton. But he did not dare refuse this strange apparition, so he agreed. The skeleton and the boy wrestled back and forth, up and down the room, until the boy was gasping for breath. Remembering a trick his older brother had taught him, he twisted suddenly and threw the skeleton onto the ground. The skeleton's leg fell off, but it just laughed, stuck its leg back on and said: "You've won! Such courage deserves a reward. Come, I will give you my treasure."

The boy was startled. What kind of treasure could an old skeleton have?

"Pick me up and carry me on your back to the next room," said the skeleton. "Remember to take your candle."

The boy picked up the skeleton and put it on his back. Then he retrieved his candle from the corner of the room and carried the skeleton into the next room. As they passed through the doorway, the skeleton blew out the candle. The boy was annoyed.

"Now, stop that," he said. The skeleton cackled madly. The boy lit the candle again, and the skeleton blew it out.

"I'm going to drop you," he threatened. He lit the candle again, and again the skeleton blew it out.

The boy dropped the skeleton onto the floor. "You'd better quit, or I will break all your bones!" he said.

"You're no fun," complained the skeleton. "But since you are so courageous and strong, I will let you see my treasure."

The boy lit the candle and turned to look at the room. From floor to ceiling, it was filled with piles and piles of gold

THE SKELETON

and silver and jewels. His legs gave way, and he sat down with a thump next to the skeleton.

"Not bad for just an old skeleton!" it laughed. Then it grew serious. "Son," it said, "I want you to promise me something."

The boy drew his gaze reluctantly from the magnificent treasure and looked at the skeleton. "What do you want me to promise?" he asked.

"I want you to promise me that you will gather all the poor people you can find in one day and give them each a bag of money. The rest you can keep for yourself."

The boy thought about this for a moment. It would be a good thing to share this wealth with the needy, he decided, so he agreed to do what the skeleton had asked.

The skeleton gave a happy laugh, jumped up, and bowed to him.

"Farewell then. Use it well."

The skeleton began to disappear, piece by piece. First his head, then his leg, then his chest, then his other leg and so on, until he was gone.

The boy gathered up the treasure, and the next day he distributed bags of coins to the poor, just as he had promised. When he had finished his task, he took the rest of the treasure back to his family, and they lived in comfort all of their days.

27

The Black Cats' Message

AUSTIN, TEXAS

I came home late one night after work and found my wife, Ethel, puttering about the kitchen with a big yellow cat at her heels.

"And who is this?" I asked jovially.

"This is our new cat," said Ethel, giving me a hug and a kiss to welcome me home. "She just appeared at the kitchen door and wanted to come in. None of the neighbors know where she came from, so I guess she's ours. It will be nice to have some company around the house."

I bent down and scratched the yellow cat under the chin. She purred and stretched.

"Well, I think our income can stretch far enough to feed three," I said.

My son had taken over my job at the mercantile, and my wife and I were enjoying a leisurely old age. I liked to keep busy, though, and so I spent a few hours every day cutting and hauling wood to be used at the mill.

I went out to milk the cow, and when I came back in, Ethel gave the cat some cream in a saucer.

We sat on the porch after dinner, and the cat sat with us.

"You are a very nice kitty," I said to her. She purred loudly.

"Donald," Ethel said. She sounded worried. I turned to look at her. "The neighbors acted rather oddly when I told them about the cat. They seemed to think she was a ghost or a witch of some sort, transformed into a cat. They told me to get rid of her."

"A witch?" I asked, and laughed heartily. "Are you a witch, little cat?"

The cat yawned and stretched. Reluctantly, Ethel started to laugh with me. It seemed such a ludicrous notion. We sat watching the beautiful sunset, then took ourselves to bed.

The cat quickly became an essential part of our household. She would purr us awake each day and wait for cream when I brought in the morning's milking. She followed Ethel around, supervising her work during the day, and sat by the fire at night while we read aloud.

The days became shorter as autumn approached, and often I would work until nearly sunset, cutting and hauling wood. One night in October, I didn't finish hauling my last load until dusk. As soon as I had piled the last log, I started down the road, hoping to get home before dark since I had not brought a lantern with me. I rounded a corner and saw a group of black cats standing in the middle of the road. They were nearly invisible in the growing dark.

As I drew nearer, I saw that they were carrying a stretcher between them. I stopped and rubbed my eyes. That was impossible, my brain told me. But when I looked again, the stretcher was still there, and there was a little dead cat lying on it.

THE BLACK CATS' MESSAGE

I was astonished. *It must be a trick of the light,* I thought. Then one of the cats called out, "Sir, please tell Aunt Kan that Polly Grundy is dead."

My mouth dropped open in shock. I shook my head hard, not believing my ears. *How ridiculous,* I thought. *Cats don't talk.*

I hurried past the little group, carefully looking the other way. *I must be working too hard,* I thought. But I couldn't help wondering who Aunt Kan might be. And why did the cat want me to tell her Polly Grundy was dead? Was Polly Grundy the cat on the stretcher?

Suddenly, I was confronted by a small black cat standing directly before me. I stopped and looked down at it. It looked back at me with large green eyes that seemed to glow in the fading light.

"I have a message for Aunt Kan," the cat said. "Tell her that Polly Grundy is dead."

The cat stalked passed me and went to join the other cats grouped around the stretcher.

I was completely nonplussed. This was getting very spooky. Talking cats and a dead Polly Grundy. And who was Aunt Kan? I hurried away as fast as I could walk. Around me, the woods were getting darker and darker. I did not want to stay in that woods with a group of talking cats. Not that I really believed the cats had spoken. It was all a strange, waking dream brought on by too much work.

Behind me, the cats gave a strange shriek and called out together: "Old man! Tell Aunt Kan that Polly Grundy is dead!"

I'd had enough. I sprinted for home as fast as I could go and didn't stop until I had reached the safety of my porch. I paused to catch my breath. I did not want to explain to Ethel that I was seeing and hearing impossible things. She would dose me with caster oil and call the doctor.

When I was sufficiently composed, I went into the house and tried to act normally. I should have known it wouldn't work. Ethel and I had been married for thirty years, and she knew me inside and out. She didn't say anything until after I'd finished the chores. Then she sat me down in front of the fire and brought me my supper. After I'd taken a few bites and started to relax, she said, "Tell me all about it, Donald."

"I don't want to worry you," I said, reluctant to talk about what I had seen and heard on the way home.

The yellow cat was lying by the fire. She looked up when she heard my voice and came to sit by my chair. I offered her a morsel of food, which she accepted daintily.

"I'll worry more if you don't tell me," said Ethel.

"I think maybe something is wrong with my brain," I said slowly. "While I was walking home, I thought I saw some black cats carrying a stretcher with a dead cat on it. Then I thought I heard the cats talking to me. They asked me to tell Aunt Kan that Polly Grundy was dead."

The yellow cat leaped up onto the windowsill. "Polly Grundy is dead?" she cried. "Then I am the Queen of the Witches!"

She switched her tail, and the window flew open with a bang. The yellow cat leaped through it and disappeared into the night, never to return.

Ethel had to dump an entire bucket of water over my head to revive me from my faint.

"The good news," she told me when I sat up, dripping and swearing because the water was ice cold, "is that you have nothing wrong with your brain. The bad news is that our cat has just left us to become the Queen of the Witches. We'll have to get another cat."

"Oh no," I said immediately. "I've had enough of cats."

We got a dog.

28

Pedro de Urdemalas

LOS ALAMOS, NEW MEXICO

Oh my! That Pedro de Urdemalas! What a bad man he was! He spent all his life swindling his employers, tricking honest folks into giving him meals, and wheedling people into paying his debts. Sometimes he walked about dressed as a beggar so that people would give him alms. It was one of these times that he did his only good deed.

Pedro was traveling down the road toward Los Alamos in New Mexico when he stumbled upon a poor old beggar man who was in rags worse than the ones Pedro was wearing. Pedro felt badly for such a fellow, and when the man begged for alms, Pedro gave him all the money in his pocket. Well, this poor beggar man happened to be Saint Peter in disguise. He asked Pedro how he might reward him. Thinking this was a joke between beggars, Pedro asked for a pack of cards that would never lose, a flute and drum that would make people dance until he said stop, and a large greasewood bush into which he could throw his creditors and not release them until they forgave his debts.

"Those are very worldly wishes," said the disguised Saint Peter. "Do you have any heavenly ones?"

Pedro considered the matter and then said, "When I knock on the pearly gates, I want Saint Peter to let me in, no matter what."

"Done," said the old beggar, transforming into the tall, white-robed figure of Saint Peter.

So that wicked Pedro de Urdemalas gambled with his magic cards in every town he came to until all the good men were broke. He played the fiddle and made everyone dance while he emptied their pockets of money and jewels. And whenever creditors came after him, Pedro threw them into the greasewood bush, where they lay in discomfort until they forgave his debts.

When it came time for Pedro to die, he met Death with a pack of cards in his hands. They played a round with the magic cards, gambling for Pedro's life, and Pedro won another ten years. After ten years, Death came back. He refused to gamble again, but when Pedro asked for a song, Death permitted him to play the magic fiddle. Pedro played and Death danced for so long that finally he promised Pedro another ten years of life to secure his release. After another ten years, Death returned. Pedro was standing beside the greasewood bush, waiting for him. But Death was on his guard. He avoided the greasewood bush and grabbed Pedro by the neck. Then Death marched Pedro down to purgatory because he had been so bad.

Pedro de Urdemalas looked about purgatory for a while and decided it wasn't so bad. He quickly became the boss and would whip all the souls who tried to defy his wishes. One soul escaped to heaven and told God what was happening in purgatory.

PEDRO DE URDEMALAS

God was annoyed with Pedro and had him sent to limbo.

Pedro de Urdemalas looked about limbo for a while and decided it would make a nice home if it weren't for all the unbaptized babies calling "Water! Water!" as they floated about. To get some peace and quiet, Pedro rounded up the babies and tossed them into the river. They popped right back up as baptized souls and flew straight to heaven. Now God was really annoyed with Pedro for causing so much trouble in limbo. So God sent him to hell.

On his way down the long hot road to hell, Pedro collected a bunch of crosses and other holy relics. As soon as he entered hell, all the demons ran from the crosses and relics as fast as they could go. But clever Pedro de Urdemalas had nailed them over all the doors and windows. The demons clustered into the middle of hell, wailing worse than the tormented souls. The devil finally escaped through the chimney and went right to heaven to complain to God.

God was very angry now. He ordered an angel to bring Pedro to the gates of heaven. As soon as they reached heaven, Pedro ran right up to the pearly gates and knocked. Saint Peter appeared. Pedro de Urdemalas said, "Let me in, Saint Peter, just as you promised." So Saint Peter had to let him in.

God had had enough of Pedro de Urdemalas. "Pedro," he said, "I am going to turn you into a rock."

"A rock with eyes," Pedro said quickly, and God agreed.

So Pedro de Urdemalas became a rock with eyes, and he stands to this day just inside the pearly gates and watches the new souls entering heaven.

29

The Lady in Blue

ISLETA, NEW MEXICO

I came into the house with an armful of blue flowers I had picked for my mama. She was in the kitchen making dinner, and she looked up at me with a smile.

"Happy birthday, Mama," I said shyly.

"Why, Sammy, how nice!" she exclaimed, reaching into the cupboard to get a vase. We arranged them carefully and put the flowers in the center of the kitchen table.

"Did you see the Blue Lady?" Mama asked, as she poured me a glass of milk and set a small plate of cookies in front of me.

"Who?" I asked, munching.

"The Blue Lady," Mama said. "She is the spirit of Maria Coronel de Agreda, who watches over the unfortunate. Wherever she steps, blue flowers appear."

"Does she wear a blue dress?" I asked. "And does she have a pretty face with a gentle smile?"

Mama looked at me in astonishment. I blushed furiously. "A nice lady showed me where to find these flowers. I didn't have enough money to buy the flowers I wanted at the florist.

The lady was on the sidewalk as I came out of the shop. She asked me why I looked so sad. When I told her about your birthday, she sent me to pick these flowers for you. She was wearing a blue dress, and she spoke to me in Spanish."

Mama laid a hand over her heart. "*Madre de Dios!* Could it be the Blue Lady?" she gasped. She stared in amazement at the flowers. "Yes, I believe she would stop and help a little boy trying to do something special for his mama," she said, more to herself than to me.

"I don't understand," I said, carefully wiping the crumbs from my mouth with my napkin. "Who is she?"

"Maria Coronel de Agreda was a nun who lived in Spain back in the 1600s," Mama said, still staring at the flowers. "They say that when Padre Alonzo de Beavides first came to the Southwest, he was visited by a group of Native Americans who wanted a priest to come to their tribe to baptize them and to help them build a church. None of the white men had ever heard of this tribe before. The Padre asked them why they wanted a church, and they told him that they had been visited many times by a white lady dressed in blue. She had spoken their language and had told them all about God. They did not know where she came from or where she went when she left. They described her clothing so accurately that Padre Alonzo was sure she must have been one of the Franciscan sisters in Spain.

"The tribesmen became very excited when Padre Alonzo showed them a painting he had of a Franciscan sister. They claimed that the nun in the picture was wearing the same clothes as the Blue Lady. The Padre was amazed by their story.

THE LADY IN BLUE

He wrote to the church authorities back in Spain to ask if any women had been sent to the New World as missionaries. The church told him that no women were being sent to the New World."

"None at all?" I exclaimed.

"None at all," Mama confirmed. "Padre Alonzo did not know how to explain the stories that reached him over and over again of Native American tribes who had met the Blue Lady.

"Many years later, another Padre named Damien Manzanet was approached by a local chief who wanted to barter some vegetables and skins in exchange for a blue cloth to bury his old mother in. Padre Damien was surprised by this request. He asked the man why he wanted to bury his mother in a blue shroud, and the man explained that it was the color the beautiful white lady had worn when she baptized the members of his tribe and told them about heaven. This was many years ago, back when his mother was a young girl, the chief explained. Ever since then, the tribe had buried their dead in blue, wanting them to look like the lady when they entered heaven."

"So, how did Maria get to the New World?" I asked.

Mama smiled mysteriously. "The first Padre, Alonzo de Beavides, heard through his Spanish contacts about Maria Coronel de Agreda, who was a mother superior at a convent in Agreda. She claimed to be the Blue Lady he sought, though she almost never left her cloister. Padre Alonzo went to visit her in Spain, and Maria told him about her prayerful concern for the native tribes in the New World. She described the vivid dreams that she had of visiting the Southwest. These dreams had started in 1629. She described the scenery, the clothing and customs of many of the Native Americans, and gave him the names of individuals she had met. She was so accurate in her descriptions, that Padre Alonzo was convinced that she was the Blue Lady.

"When he asked Maria how she had communicated with the tribesmen, she told the Padre that she had spoken normally to the Native Americans, and God had let them understand her. Padre Alonzo later met some of the people she had named from her dreams.

"In 1631, after a few terrible nightmares, Maria ceased dreaming about the Southwest. The Blue Lady came no more to the Native American tribes.

"Skeptics over the years have tried to search for a rational answer, thinking that Maria must have taken leave from the convent and come to the Southwest, or sent another nun in her place, but the records showed that no nun left the convent for a period long enough to travel to the New World and back. It is a mystery.

"They say that the spirit of Maria Coronel de Agreda still visits this region, and where she steps, blue flowers appear," Mama said.

"Do you really think I met the Blue Lady, Mama?" I asked.

Mama smiled. "You certainly met *a* blue lady, Sammy. I don't know if she was the spirit of the Blue Lady or just some kind woman helping a young boy, but she certainly acted in the same gracious manner as Maria Coronel de Agreda."

30

Uncle Bob's Miracle

BRAZORIA COUNTY, TEXAS

Uncle Bob was just about the most holy man that had ever walked this earth. He was a slave who had spent most of his seventy-two years working faithfully for his master on the plantation. Every time a child got sick or a fellow had a fight with his wife, Uncle Bob would pray, and everything would be all right. There wasn't anyone who could outpray Uncle Bob.

Now, Uncle Bob was getting on in years. One day, his master told him that if Uncle Bob paid him $20, he would be free. Uncle Bob didn't have a penny to his name, but he was sure that if he prayed hard enough, God would give him the money.

Uncle Bob liked to go into the woods after dinner each night to pray. He had a special tree beneath which he always knelt and made his requests. Uncle Bob prayed for two hours that night that God would set him free. "I just need $20, Lord," Uncle Bob said. "Just $20, and I'll be free."

Each night thereafter, Uncle Bob would kneel under the tree and pray and pray and pray, "Just $20, Lord, and I'll be free."

A month passed, and Uncle Bob still had no money. But he was sure that God would provide the cash somehow. He

UNCLE BOB'S MIRACLE

kept praying every night under his special tree. Then one night the master happened along and heard Uncle Bob saying, "I need $20, Lord. Just $20, and I'll be free." The master had a devilish sense of humor, and he decided that he would have a little fun.

The next night, the master hurried down to the tree and put a $10 bill around the back. Then he climbed up to the top and waited for Uncle Bob. Around about eight o'clock, Uncle Bob trudged down the wooded path and knelt under the tree.

"I need $20, Lord. Just $20, and I'll be free."

The master spoke in a deep, ringing voice from the top of the tree. "Very well, Bob. You may have $10 toward your freedom. I have placed the money at the back of the tree."

Uncle Bob pushed himself up off his knees and hobbled to the back of the tree. There was a $10 bill! Uncle Bob hurried back to his favorite spot and knelt down again. "Thank you, Lord! Thank you! Now, if I could have another $10, Lord. Just $10, and I'll be free."

"If you come back tomorrow," the master's voice boomed from the top of the tree, "I will give you another $5 toward your freedom."

"Thank you, Lord. Thank you," said old Uncle Bob. He pocketed the money and went home.

The next day, the slaves all talked about Uncle Bob's miracle. They were singing and praising the Lord, and many of them were privately praying for the Lord to bring them some cash too. Uncle Bob had prudently not mentioned that the Lord had volunteered to give him more money that night.

That evening, the master put a $5 bill at the back of the tree and climbed to the top to wait for Uncle Bob. Right at eight o'clock, Uncle Bob trudged down the wooded pathway and knelt beneath the tree.

"I need $10, Lord. Just $10, and I'll be free," Uncle Bob prayed.

The master spoke in a deep, ringing voice from the top of the tree. "Very well, Bob. You may have another $5 toward your freedom. I have placed the money at the back of the tree."

Uncle Bob pushed himself up off his knees and hobbled to the back of the tree. There was a $5 bill! Uncle Bob hurried back to his favorite spot and knelt down again. "Thank you, Lord! Thank you!"

"If you bring the $15 back tomorrow," the master boomed from the top of the tree, "I will take the money and give you a $20 bill on the following night."

Uncle Bob considered this offer. He put the $5 bill in his pocket and folded his hands in prayer.

"I thank you kindly for the $15, Lord," Uncle Bob said. "But I reckon I'll get the last $5 some other way."

Uncle Bob hurried home, leaving his devious master sitting all alone at the top of the tree. At first, the master was furious with Uncle Bob for outwitting him. Then he started to laugh. He laughed so long and so hard that several of the slaves came running to the edge of the woods to see what phantom was causing the racket.

The next day, the master gave old Uncle Bob his freedom in exchange for the $15 "God" had so miraculously provided.

People still tell the story of Uncle Bob's miracle, but they never pray under Uncle Bob's tree at night, because they are afraid of the Laughing Ghost, who roams the woods after dark, chuckling to itself.

Resources

Anderson, Dorothy Daniels (1993). *Arizona Legends and Lore.* Phoenix, AZ: Golden West Publishers.

Boren, Kerry Ross. "Jean Baptiste: The Ghoul of Great Salt Lake" (www.prospector-utah.com/jean.htm), accessed January 28, 2004.

Botkin, B. A., ed. (1944). *A Treasury of American Folklore.* New York: Crown Publishers.

———. (1975). *A Treasury of Western Folklore.* New York: Bonanza Books.

Brewster, J. Mason (1954). *Texas Folk and Folklore.* Dallas: Southern Methodist University Press.

Cactus Jim. *The Haunted Desert* (www.desertusa .com/magoct97/octmore/oct_haunted.html), accessed September 18, 2003.

Coffin, Tristam P., and Hennig Cohen, eds. (1973). *Folklore from the Working Folk of America.* New York: Doubleday.

Craddock, John R. (1924). *Legend of Stampede Mesa.* Austin: Texas Folk-Lore Society.

Dobie, J. Frank, ed. (1924). *Legends of Texas.* Austin: Texas Folk-Lore Society.

———. (1932). *"Tone the Bell Easy."* Publications of the Texas Folk-Lore Society, Number 10. Austin: Texas Folklore Society.

———. (1933). "Spur-of-the-Cock." *Publications of the Texas Folk-Lore Society, Number XI.* Austin: Texas Folk-Lore Society.

Eckhardt, C. F. *The Mystery of the Lady in Blue.* (www.texfiles .com/eckhardt/ladyinblue.htm), accessed January 25, 2004.

Erdoes, Richard, and Alfonso Ortiz (1984). *American Indian*

Myths and Legends. New York: Pantheon Books.

Espinosa, José Manuel (1937). *Spanish Folk-Tales from New Mexico*. New York: G. E. Stechert & Co.

Glassock, C. B. (1932). *Gold in Them Hills*. Indianapolis: Bobbs-Merrill Co.

Hallenbeck, Cleve, and J. H. William (1938). *Legends of the Spanish Southwest*. Glendale, CA: Arthur H. Clark Co.

Hand, Wayland D. (1942). *California Miners' Folklore: Below Ground* Vol. 1, Number 2. California: California Folklore Quarterly.

Ison, Yvette D. (1995). "Unsolved Mysteries in Utah—The Bizarre Case of Grave Robber Jean Baptiste." *History Blazer* (historytogo.utah.gov/mystery.html), accessed January 28, 2004.

Martin, MaryJoy. *Phantoms of the Rails* (gorp.away.com /gorp/publishers/pruett/phantoms.htm), accessed January 4, 2004.

Paher, Stanley W., ed. (1981). *Nevada Towns & Tales*, Vol. 1: North. Las Vegas: Nevada Publications.

Peck, Catherine, ed. (1998). *A Treasury of North American Folk Tales*. New York: W. W. Norton.

Polley, J., ed. (1978). *American Folklore and Legend*. New York: Reader's Digest Association.

Rich, Joseph C. (1868). "The Bear Lake Monster." *Deseret News* (bearlake.dcdi.net/bearlakemonster.htm), accessed April 4, 2002.

Rumble, L. (1993). *Annals Australasia*. Kingston, New South Wales: Chevalier Press.

Schlosser, Sandra E. (2002). *The Dance* (www.american folklore.net/folktales/tx3.html), accessed April 15, 2002.

Skinner, Charles M. (1896). *Myths and Legends of Our Own Land,* Vol. 2. Philadelphia: J. B. Lippincott.

———. (1903). *American Myths and Legends,* Vol. 2. Philadelphia: J. B. Lippincott.

Taylor, Troy (2003). "Haunted Utah." *The Legend of John Baptiste* (www.prairieghosts.com/baptiste.html), accessed January 28, 2004.

Weiser, Kathy, ed. (1998). "Legends of America." *Buckskin Joe, Colorado* (www.legendsofamerica.com/CP-BuckskinJoe2 .html), accessed February 1, 2004.

Wilson, Rufus Rockwell (1936). *Out of the West.* New York: Press of the Pioneers.

Young, Richard, and Judy Dockery (1991). *Ghost Stories from the American Southwest.* Little Rock, AR: August House Publishers.

About the Author

S. E. Schlosser has been telling stories since she was a child, when games of "let's pretend" quickly built themselves into full-length stories acted out with friends. A graduate of the Institute of Children's Literature and Rutgers University, she created and maintains the Web site AmericanFolklore.net, where she shares a wealth of stories from all fifty states, some dating back to the origins of America. Sandy spends much of her time answering questions from visitors to the site. Many of her favorite e-mails come from other folkorists who delight in practicing the old tradition of who can tell the tallest tale.